To: Sue

Live free

Love

Sandra Lunden

Read my story

millie Rytel

11-15-2012

D1082445

FOUR CONTINENTS
TO FREEDOM

A
Biography
of
Millie Rytel

by
Sandra Lundin

Published by Jupiter4Press
P.O. Box 334, Schererville, Indiana 46375
Email jupiter4press@sbcglobal.net
www.jupiter4press.cc
Published in cooperation with Lightning Source Publishing Inc and in arrangement with Sandra Lundin, July 23, 2007

The contents of this book are a biography of Millie Zygmunt Rytel written by Sandra Lundin.

Cover by Michael Blackett
Four Continents to Freedom

━━━━━━━━━━

This is a true story. However, the dialogue and letters were reconstructed from Millie's (and her family's) memory of events that occurred as much as 85 years ago.

This journey passed through many countries with different languages and/or alphabets. Therefore there may be more than one spelling for some geographical names.

Over the last 85 years the political boundaries in Europe, Asia and Africa have experienced many changes.

Those who cannot remember the past are condemned to repeat it.

George Santayana, 1905

Let me be an agent for change whenever I see injustice.

Prayer spoken in
Our Saviour Lutheran Church,
Lansing, IL
2005

ACKNOWLEDGMENTS

I would like to extend my thanks and gratitude to:

My encouraging friends, Wally and Sue Fulton. As a life coach, Sue helps her clients attain their life goals. Wally is a high school and junior college rhetoric and English teacher, who won the 1984 Illinois Governor's Master Teacher of the Year award. He constructively edited the first three drafts of this book.

My writers' groups, Village Writers and Write-On Hoosiers, for their encouragement and willingness to share their literary expertise. I am especially grateful to Fred Boling, John Achor, Madelyn Young, Katherine Flotz, Michael Blackett and Sharon Palmeri.

The four engineers and one chemist who described the steelmaking industry. Three of these men had fathers who were steelworkers in the 1930's and 1940's, and they understand both the technical and physical nature of the steel manufacturing. They have asked not to be named.

My friend Jacque Hamers, a counselor who gave the professional advice: "It will lessen Millie's pain to tell her story." Jacque also orchestrated *Nizhnya Striga,* from Millie's tape recording.

Nina Hoogewerf, who grew up in the Russian republic of Belarus, for translating the song *Nizhnya*

Striga, as Millie sang it, and for editing the Glossary of Russian words.

Edward Barton, the Youth Ministry Director at Woodmar Methodist Church, for his help with a computer program printing the music and words of *Nizhnya Striga.*

Wesley Adamczyk, for his assistance with the history of the Katyn Massacre and Russian deportation of Polish citizens.

Jan Loris, Director of the Polish Museum, for his help with Polish history.

My children and grandchildren for their encouragement, and especially my husband, Don, for his patient support and love.

And to Millie, Lottie and Lucille, who lived "Four Continents to Freedom" and were willing to tell their story.

INDEX

Photos:

Maps:

Music:

Glossary

A BRIEF

Sandra Lundin, at the age of 12, won a county essay contest for elementary school children, and she was hooked on writing. All four of her children entered school speech contests for which she wrote the monologues.

She is grateful to her neighbor, Mille, who trusted Sandra to write the story of two betrayals. She lives with her husband in Highland, Indiana and Hot Springs Village, Arkansas.

*   *   *   *   *   *   *   *

Mille Rytel kept the pain of her abduction into Siberian slavery inside her head for 60 years until she bonded with her neighbor. While this manuscript chronicles distressful times, it also shows the Polish uplifting spirit, determination – and humor.

She says this book is a labor of love for her daughters and grandchildren. But also important to Millie, she hopes that "Four Continents to Freedom" will help curb any injustices that might otherwise occur in our world.

1

GOOD LIFE IN
SOUTHEAST POLAND

1920

Dear Mother and Father and sisters,

We love America, but we miss our family in Poland. We think of you all the time. Both Ignatc and I have good jobs. We have found an apartment here in Chicago. We each have a bedroom, and there is a parlor and a big kitchen and a bathroom with a bathtub.

We are inviting any of our four sisters, Appolonia, Stephanie, Ann, and Sophie, to come to America. You can stay with us. There are plenty of jobs. Our bosses ask us if we know any more Polish people they can hire because we are all such good workers.

The Polish bachelors in America far outnumber the single ladies. When you get to Chicago, you will have your pick of many suitors. Now that the other men found out about our four sisters in Poland, they want to be our friends so they can be the first to meet our sisters as soon as you arrive here. If you decide to come, let us know in a letter and we will take care of your transportation. We hope to see you soon.

Love, Stanley and Ignatc

The letter from Stanley and Ignatc had a power far beyond its two pages. Eggs were left ungathered from the hen's nest – burning bread was forgotten in the oven – cows found an open gate and made their way onto the road – as the members of the Majka family scurried to the kitchen to read and absorb the information from America.

"I'm going," decided Appolonia as she was already considering what to pack.

Ann and Sophie were still teenagers not yet confident about the world, and they decided to stay in Poland.

Stephanie wasn't so sure. "I'll have to talk to Walter before I decide."

* * * * * * * *

Millie Zygmunt Rytel is my name, and with the help of OTHER VOICES, this book is my life story.

On a farm near Niwiska in southern Poland, my mother, Stephanie Majka, was born on April 17, 1902, when this area was under Austrian control. After fathering six children, my grandmother's first husband died. When she remarried, my grandmother had six more children, and my mother, Stephanie, was the fourth of those six. Their centuries-old house had one great room with a dirt floor, which was polished every week with a special liquid. The parents occupied one small bedroom, and all the children slept in the other. Both of my grandmother's two families were very poor, and there were few opportunities for young people in Niwiska.

Having six brothers and sisters share one small bedroom must have been intolerable for grandmother's first family. With their mother's second husband and new babies crowding into the house, most of Stephanie's stepsisters and stepbrothers must have had an incentive to move out. Some of them emigrated from Poland to America.

After the end of World War I in 1918, Stephanie's two full brothers, Stanley and Ignatc, followed their stepbrothers to the United States. The Polish American bachelors they met encouraged one another to bring more Polish young women to America.

In Poland at that time, there was a tradition of matchmaking whereby, if the wealth of the families of two young people was similar, the girl's parents could then offer a dowry to the boy's family. Their finances were more important than any other quality of the young person. Coming from a poor household, Appolonia, Stephanie's older sister, had no prospects in the old country, so she joined her brothers in Chicago, where she soon met her husband and moved to Hammond, Indiana.

*   *   *   *   *   *   *   *

My father, Walter Zygmunt, the youngest in a family of two boys and three girls, was born on February 21, 1901, in a big home in the town of Niwiska near his parents' large farm. His mother employed a maid, and his father was able to hire extra farm hands at harvest time. These were signs that they were probably the wealthiest family in the area.

When Walter was eleven or twelve years old, both his parents died. Walter's older brother farmed the land, and my father became the main cook for the family and for the farm workers they hired. He was an excellent cook.

By the end of World War I, Walter was living in the family home with his brother and sister-in-law when the Russian Bolsheviks invaded Poland. He joined a Polish unit of volunteers who were known as the Blue Army because of the color of their uniforms. Led by General Haller, this army also recruited many volunteers from other countries, like France and America, to fight the aggressors in this Battle of Poland.

In what became known as the Miracle of the Vistulas, against great odds this unofficial army defeated the Bolsheviks and pushed them back into Russia. Walter served for two years until 1920, when he came back to Niwiska to court my mother. Although he could have attracted a wealthier girl with a dowry, he knew he loved Stephanie. Walter told her, "When we played together as children, I liked you better than any other girl. As you grew into a young lady, I knew I wanted to be with you always."

Although he wasn't too tall, Walter was such a good handsome guy that all the girls were interested in him. They tried to make my mother jealous. I remember my mother saying, "I was lucky to have a faithful fiancé like Walter. I knew he loved me and wouldn't be swayed by all those girls."

As a veteran, my father was allowed to buy a

Photo #1

Walter (left) in uniform in - 1922

large acreage in eastern Poland from General Haller at a special low price, which was subsidized by the grateful Polish nation. These 50 acres were as much as he could afford. "This amount of land is bigger than the farms around here," Walter told his fiancé. "With this much good ground, we will have enough income to support ourselves for the rest of our lives and to take care of any children we have. This is a wonderful opportunity. We'll do better here in Poland than we would if we went to America."

"And," Stephanie added, "this means we won't have to start over learning English."

It was an easy decision for the two lovers. Of course they would stay in Poland and buy the large farm. They would not go to America. In 1921 my parents were married in the large old church in their village.

Because their new farm was in Hallerczyn, near the larger town of Lwow, in the southeastern part of Poland, Walter and Stephanie moved far away almost to the border of Ukraine, which was then a republic of Russia. One result of this move was that they didn't communicate as much with their families, and they totally lost contact with Stephanie's three American siblings.

In Poland at that time, every male was required to serve for two years in his nation's army, and he was not respected as a man until he fulfilled this duty. Even though Walter had fought with General Haller, this did not satisfy Father's military commitment, and he was drafted into the Polish army.

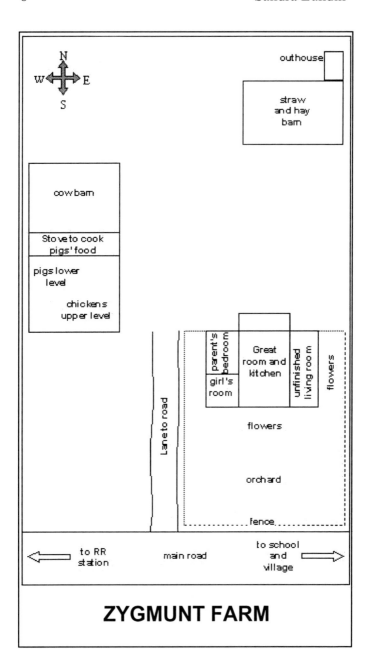

In 1922, Stephanie gave birth to a baby girl, who died at the age of six months while Walter was in the service. My sister Wladyslawa (later changed to Lottie) was born in 1924. I was named Mieczyslawa (which was changed to Millie) when I was born on November 22, 1926, and my sister Lucille joined our family in 1928. Then in 1934 my mother gave birth to another girl named Teresa, who was always sickly.

Walter built a new brick, tile-roofed house when, as newlyweds, he and Stephanie moved to Hallerczyn. Because they were always short of money, only three rooms were finished. The living room was never completed. We had a large kitchen, the parent's bedroom and one bedroom shared by the three daughters. All three of us slept in one bed, with one of us lying crosswise on the bottom. When we grew older, we raced to get into bed first because the third girl would have to sleep on a thin mattress on the floor. In the summertime we put a blanket over some fresh hay for our soft summer mattress. When Teresa became old enough, she slept on a small cot in the corner of our bedroom.

My father and mother were affectionate toward each other, and they were good parents to their four daughters. They made sure their children ate good food and lived in a warm house. Whenever I had a problem, they were there to listen and to help me find a solution, and the hugs and kisses were common around our house. They were also very strict, and when my father gave an order like, "Do your homework, and do it now," he expected to be obeyed. As a mischievous small child, I can remember crying when I was spanked, and thereafter the threat of a licking was always there.

During the summer from early in the morning until the sun went down, my father spent most of his time walking in the field behind the plow. He raised wheat and barley, as well as sugar beets, and Mother tended a vegetable garden where she grew most of our food. She also helped Father with the farm work, and my sisters and I did too, whenever we could.

On any given day, one of us would feed the chickens, another would slop the pigs, and the third girl would pitch hay to the eight cows. We also owned two horses, about ten turkeys and dozens of geese and ducks, as well as two dogs and a bunch of cats. The cats were good for farms because they kept the mice under control. The dogs were kept tied up at their kennel, and like good watchdogs, they barked whenever a stranger came onto our property.

Our farm had an orchard with pear and apple trees, as well as many varieties of cherries, including bing cherries. We three daughters climbed those trees to harvest the fruit, all the while eating as much as we wanted. I can remember eating so much fruit that I couldn't eat supper.

"Millie is hiding in the tree again," my sisters would tell our parents. "She doesn't want to eat supper."

My father was a knowledgeable horticulturalist, and he grafted as many as five different apple varieties onto one tree. We also raised strawberries in a garden, and of course my sisters and I weeded those patches and picked the berries. All this fruit ripened on a varying schedule, with the strawberries coming early in the summer, then cherries, and then the various apple varieties were harvested over a period of months. Put into boxes cushioned with straw and stored in the ground, the apples lasted all winter.

We made money selling milk to the dairy. Father kept the milk cold in the summertime by pouring it into a clean tank, which he then lowered on ropes down into the cold water of our well. The dairyman picked up the milk, separated out the cream, which he kept, and returned the skim milk to us to feed our pigs.

My parents hatched their own chicks and ducklings in incubators located in a special well-insulated barn room, which was heated with a coal and wood stove. The barn, which Father built, had an area for cows and one for pigs. Above the pigs' section was a chicken house with a small ladder for the laying hens to walk up to their individual coops where they laid their eggs. These were free-range chickens, and during the summer months they might lay their eggs outdoors. As far back as I can remember, mother would tell us, "Follow the hens and gather their eggs as soon as they lay them."

Father's main cash income came from raising hogs for bacon. He closely watched these pigs because they couldn't be too fat or too skinny. Their food was a formula of potatoes and grains like oats, which we cooked on the stove in their barn. When they were eight months old, he delivered them to a butcher in the next town, who made up a classification system for these animals. When my father came home after selling his pigs, we all ran to meet him.

"What grade did you get for your pigs this year?"

"It was a first class rating. What did you think it would be?" he answered.

We were excited because this meant more money for the whole family, plus a bonus of lard for Mother's baking and candy for us to eat.

During the winter my father let the cows and pigs out of their barn so they could exercise in our farmyard. He did this when it was very cold, because he knew they wouldn't wander away. They always scurried back through the open door of the barn when they got cold.

The straw on the ground in the animal barn was changed every few days, after which it was saved for fertilizing the fields. Father stored two kinds of straw in a separate barn called a *stodola*. The coarser straw was for the roofs of the barns and the better kind was fed to the animals.

When the crops were ripe in the fall, father hired extra workers to help because harvesting was heavy work that only strong men could do. Mother cooked breakfast, lunch and dinner for the harvest people, because on a farm in the old country the first thing you needed to do was feed the laborers.

Mother worked hard with the cooking, but she had a dishwasher. Actually she had three: Lottie, Millie, and Lucille.

"I hate washing these big cooking pots," we grumbled, but not loud enough for our parents to hear. That would not be a good idea, we had learned the hard way. All the dish and clothes washing was done on an enclosed porch. Because our house had no running water, we had to carry it from the well outside, which made washing on Mondays difficult. My mother soaked the clothes in a big barrel overnight so the dirt would come off easily the next morning when she scrubbed them by hand on a portable washboard. My sisters and I hung up the clothes outside, and by the time they were dry, the sun was setting.

Our house had no bathtub. When we were small, Mother heated the water on the stove and poured it into a big barrel, which the three of us would climb into at same time to take our bath. "There was a lot of splashing and fighting," my mother often reminded us. "By the time you three were clean, there was more water on the floor than in the tub."

All of us worked hard, but we enjoyed good food because my mother was an excellent cook. We waited for her daily home-baked bread to come out of the oven so we could eat it hot with homemade butter. When Mother brought food to potluck suppers, she beamed when people who tasted her food said, "Mrs. Zygmunt, you are the best cook in the whole village."

For two weeks at Christmas time Mother baked all kinds of special pastries like butter and sugar cookies, cheesecakes, *chrusciki* (braided raisin bread), and honey cake. My father took care of a neighbor's beehive so we could have access to honey. Mother gave her pastries to other families around the village.

Everyone, including the mailman and the policemen, knew they could stop and visit during the holiday season. All the neighbors and friends would be invited for informal open houses. Of course, everyone brought their children, and the kids entertained themselves by singing or playing games. If we disturbed the adults and their card playing, we were told, "Go to your room and play there." We liked that better anyway, because then we could make more noise.

The Christmas season planning started with buying firewood. There were no trees near our farm, and Father traveled to a forest about twenty miles away to buy logs, which were expensive. In the fall after all the crops were in, he made several trips with a horse and wagon to buy enough wood to get us through the winter heating season. After Father got home, he chopped the firewood into smaller, usable pieces. It was then stored in a dry shed so that Mother would have fuel for her baking.

There was planning involved in baking. First, a lot of wood was burned before the stove was hot enough for Mother to put the bread or pastries into the oven with her wooden shovel, which she coated with flour. She peeked into the oven to make sure the bread was just the right stage of doneness before she took it out. It was hard work, but mother described her labor by saying, "This is how I show love to my family."

During the long winter months, father borrowed books from the area library. In the evenings he invited any of his neighbors who wanted to come, and he read to the group from the classics or historical novels he selected. Mother also liked to read, but her choice ran to romances.

On any farm all kids were needed to help with the chores, but life wasn't all work. Both my mother and father were always showing affection to their children. They were fair and loving, often hugging and kissing us. We were lucky with our upbringing because our activities and education always interested our parents. Their rule was, "Your school work comes first."

Rain or shine or snow, we walked three miles to and from school down a dusty or muddy farm road. "You're going to school today," Mother said, "and there will be no discussion."

During the winter when it snowed more than six inches, my father took us to school on a horse-drawn sled. When it snowed during our school day we'd whisper to one another, "I hope it snows enough for father to come with the sled."

I liked school, both for the learning and for playing with friends. During recess and lunchtime we played games like hopscotch, basketball and volleyball. We also had a game similar to tennis that we made up, using a string for a net, and balls and racquets brought from home by any kid who had them.

There were three rooms in our school: First, second and third grades were in one room, then fifth and sixth, and seventh and eighth. About eight kids were in each grade. We learned writing, reading, history and Polish. In the second grade we began studying Ukrainian, which was very much like Russian. That was the law because many people of Ukrainian descent were Polish citizens.

My parents were friendly with all their new neighbors, but they missed their families in

Niwiska. The only relatives who lived in Hallerczyn were my father's cousin and his family of two boys and two girls, the oldest of whom was named Mary. I don't remember if their family or ours moved to the area first. We spent holiday gatherings with them, and we played with their children. Hopscotch, hide and seek, and tag were our favorite outdoor games. During the winter we played musical chairs and card games like war. We made up a game called secret where we sat in a row and the first kid in line whispered a message to the second and so on. By the time the secret reached the last person, we would all laugh at the garbled message.

Our cousins' land bordered our farm with just a gated wooden fence between us. They raised ducks and chickens and we did too. The poultry didn't care where the boundary was; they ate wherever they happened to be at the time. Our properties were separated, but the ducks didn't know it. Mary's family had a big orchard with trees loaded with plums, which they would dry into prunes. With permission, we went across the fence and picked plums to eat whenever we wanted. As kids we stole each other's fruit, which we ate right off the trees without washing, because in those days there was no such thing as poison spray.

I grew up admiring Mary, our neighbor's oldest daughter, who was about seven years older than I was. She walked to the train every weekday to go to teachers college in the town of Brody, always wearing a nice coat and hat. She carried a briefcase for her college papers. I liked her stylish, professional appearance. As children, we helped on the farm so we were not often dressed up. I said,

"I'd like to be like Marisha (Mary). I want an education too."

At the age of fourteen, my sister Lottie started her first year of high school at a neighboring town about seven miles away. With his horse and wagon, father drove her to school on Monday morning and she boarded with a friend until Friday. I idolized both Lottie and Mary.

My sisters and I made friends with Father's cousin, who was old enough that we called her Grandma. We helped her with little chores, and in return she invited us to play in her house. She had a lot of room, something we didn't have at home. I suppose she liked our company, because she would call, "Hey kids, come over to my house. I have some cookies for you," and we ran right over.

My parents also made friends with Polish citizens of Ukrainian descent, whom they first met when they moved to eastern Poland. One particular friend was a handsome man who became like a brother to my father. They were always helping each other. "May I borrow your hoe?" his friend might ask, and my father never refused him. When working a field bordering our farm, this Ukrainian's family often came to our house to ask, "Will you give us a drink of water?" Sometimes they ate with us.

Although they were Eastern Orthodox and we were Catholic, we exchanged visits to each other's churches. On holidays, if we didn't have church, we attended their *cerkief*. We even received communion from their priest. When we attended the Orthodox Church, we followed their rituals. We knelt, kissed the ground and made three crosses. We said, "*mioca ducha switoho*. Amen." (Father, Son, and Holy Ghost.)

The Polish and Ukrainian children also made friends. Children all over the world don't care about each other's background; they just want to have fun and enjoy one another.

There were some bad feelings in the area between these two ethnic groups of Polish citizens, perhaps because most of the Ukrainians were poorer with smaller farms and larger families. Their houses had very small windows and thatched roofs, while our home was brick with a roof of tile.

Although there was some tension, everyone got along because they were close neighbors. All of us lived in peace, or so we thought.

Our calm world would soon be shattered by people we didn't even know.

2

GERMANY AND RUSSIA INVADE POLAND

World War II began for us without any warning. Germany invaded Poland from the north and west on September 1, 1939, and soon their planes were flying overhead in our skies. Poland then declared war on Germany. When Mother was shopping in the village, the store owner told her, "German dive-bombing planes shot some kids playing at a park."

"Do you believe this happened?" she asked my father.

"We can't prove it one way or the other," he replied. "But we should take no chances and stay hidden when the planes fly over."

Because our school hadn't started that fall, we were all at home during the day. After that rumor circulated, no one needed to be told to stay even closer to the house. Whenever someone heard a plane overhead, she yelled "plane" and we all ran for cover.

Three days after the invasion, at the age of 38, my father was called to serve in the Polish army for the third time. He left us on the farm with the potatoes not yet dug and the beets still in the field. Mother called a meeting with her daughters. "Girls, your father isn't here to get the crops from the field before the freezing weather comes, so we have to bring in the harvest. I'll hire a couple of farm laborers to help, but all of us must work hard all day or we won't have food to eat this winter."

The weather that September was dry and warm – perfect for working outside. Lottie and I turned over the ground in the fields by hitching the horse to the plow. Lottie held the plow handles behind the horse, while I pulled and whipped the horse from the front. In that way, we prepared the fields for the next year before the cold weather set in. Perhaps it was a good thing that we needed to work, because we were too tired at night to lie awake worrying about father fighting in the war.

I can recall my mother saying, "The war will be over soon, and we can get back to normal. It will get better."

It got worse.

I remember a neighbor bursting through our front door.

"Stephanie, Russian soldiers are in our town robbing everything in the stores and in the houses. Put your money in a safe place, and hide your food or they will steal it all."

"How can that be true?" my mother asked. "We are at war with Germany. Walter is at the western front fighting the Germans, not the Russians. You must be confused."

We discovered the neighbor was not mistaken when we saw the Russian army for ourselves. There were what seemed like a million soldiers rumbling down the road past our farm with their tanks and guns. Although the main highway came right past our property, which was fenced in, for some reason the Russians left us alone. Many of our neighbors were not so lucky, and they lost almost all their livestock and any food that was not hidden. In the village, the bakery and grocery store were the first places that were laid bare. Dry goods stores and jewelry shops were next to be stripped of all their merchandise.

The soldiers were so poor that they didn't know what a watch looked like. They were so hungry they would catch and cook any animal they saw. Stealing food when you are starving isn't arrogance. It's surviving. They did what any hungry person would do – steal.

In Russia, hams and sausages would be hanging in the stores, but upon looking closely, anyone could see that everything was wooden. Most of their citizens had been forced into communes, which were so unproductive that even their people living on the land didn't have enough food to eat. The war was just starting so Poland was still pretty rich in food and other goods. Or we were, until the Russians grabbed anything and everything they wanted.

Under any other circumstances I would have said the soldiers, who looked as young as 19 or 20, were handsome. They wore heavy black boots and olive green wool uniforms with matching hats decorated with one red star, and they carried backpacks and long rifles.

For three or four days the Russian soldiers marched past our house alongside their tanks. Day and night there were hundreds of tanks passing our farm. They said, "We are here to help you fight Germany." We didn't believe this, but we were careful not to argue. When any of the soldiers asked us a question, we answered in Ukrainian. If they said, "We want some water," we ran to bring the water. We were not friendly with these invaders, but we were trying to stay out of trouble. They could have done anything they wanted, including raping or killing us, because there was no police authority to stop them.

The most terrifying thing was that we had nowhere to turn for help. All the younger men were fighting Germany. The older men still at home didn't know what to do. A neighbor whose house was robbed told us, "I tried to call the police, but it was no use because the policemen were hiding along with the rest of us. They wouldn't even admit they were policemen."

During this time we didn't leave our farm for any reason because we were afraid. Anyway, we had nowhere to go since the stores were closed for lack of goods to sell, and the new school year didn't start after Germany invaded. Then, as quickly as it appeared, the Russian army was gone because it moved off toward the west.

Being at war was a frightening time for my family, especially since Father was fighting in western Poland. We prayed for our dad to come safely home. Every night we pleaded, "Please God, keep Father safe. Send him home."

As if in answer to our prayers, my father came home at the end of September in 1939, driving a wagon pulled by two beautiful horses. All of us were shouting and crying at the same time, yelling, "It's father." Mother came running out of the house when she heard our screaming. She started yelling too, even while she grabbed her husband in a big hug.

Everyone shouted at once. "What happened?" "We are glad to see you, but how is it that you're home?" "Shouldn't you be fighting the war?" "Where did you get the horses and wagon?" "Are you all right?" "Are you hungry?"

Father laughed at his family's barrage of questions, as he told us his story. "On about September 22, I was driving an ammunition wagon to the war front, when our Polish officers told me the war was going badly for our army," he said. "We had horse-mounted guns and cavalry, while the Germans had *Stuka* dive-bomber planes, as well as trucks and tanks. Their mechanical equipment was faster and better than our horses and wagons. The officers ordered me to turn south to escape into Romania with the supplies in my wagon, but the Germans caught me a half-hour away from the Romanian border and took all my ammunition. I thought they were going to kill me."

"Instead they ordered, 'You are no threat to us without guns or ammunition. Go home and take your horses and wagon with you. We don't want them.'"

"I had no choice except to follow their instructions, because the rest of our army was already scattered throughout Romania or Poland," Father told us.

We asked more questions, "Wasn't driving an ammunition wagon a dangerous job? If you were attacked, your whole wagon would blow up, wouldn't it?"

"It wasn't as dangerous as you might think," he replied. "They told us the Germans wouldn't shoot at these wagons because they wanted to steal the ammunition, and that is what happened. When their *Stuka* dive bombers flew overhead, they never aimed at my wagon."

That evening, as we were enjoying mother's special dinner, Father wanted to know everything that happened at home while he was gone. Our celebration lasted for just that one night, however, because the next day everyone knew that Zygmunt was home from the war. When father's Ukrainian friend walked over the next day, all of us thought it was a welcome-home visit. It wasn't.

"Be careful. They want to kidnap you and kill you," his friend warned. "Stay hidden and don't let them catch you."

"Who? Who wants to do this?" my father asked.

The friend took a long time answering, "A gang of outlaw Polish Ukrainians. That's all I can say."

We knew that after the collapse of the Polish government, there was no rule of law. These ruffians ran wild and destroyed anything or anyone they hated. They hanged our local priest on a cross, cut his eyes out and slashed his throat. We would have to be careful in trusting any Ukrainian again.

"And now I have to do something to prove that I am not betraying this gang of killers by warning you," the Ukrainian friend explained, "or they will come after me."

To emphasize his words, he got into father's wagon and drove off with the two horses and everything that was in the wagon.

For four months after the warning, father spent not one more night at home. Instead he slept in barns or in the fields under the hay. When it got colder into winter he stayed at friends' homes, a different place every night. We understood what was happening and we were afraid for our father when he told us, "For your own safety, I won't tell you where I sleep at night."

Father came home for an hour or two every few days to get clean clothes and something to eat, but never at the same time of the day. I was then twelve years old and I blurted out, "Where are you staying at night?"

The only answer I could get was, "The less you know the better for everyone."

He wasn't telling mother anything either, and she was wise enough not to ask. She did question, "Are you getting enough to eat?"

Father had been warned that he was in jeopardy, but never did he ever imagine that his family was also in danger. It was the farthest thing from his mind. Walter Zygmunt was sleeping at home, a rare thing, when at 2:00 a.m. on February 10, 1940, we were rousted from our beds by the loud banging on our front door. When we opened the door…

3

KIDNAPPED TO SIBERIA

Gunpoint! A half dozen Russian soldiers, with rifles pointed at my father, pushed their way into our house. We were so startled that we couldn't believe what was happening. I started laughing because everything seemed so ridiculous, so bizarre and unreal, but my father understood immediately—this was no game.

"Millie, stop laughing. Be quiet. Don't anger the soldiers. Do whatever they tell you to do," he cautioned.

When I saw that Father was taking the soldiers seriously, a chill went through my body and I started shaking with fear.

The soldiers said, "You are going to take a trip for a few days, but this is only temporary. You will be back in your home in three or four days. You have two hours to pack whatever you want to take with you."

We wanted to believe this kidnapping would be temporary. We thought we might be held while they took all our belongings, and we expected to be released to come home to an empty house.

The soldiers could see that Teresa, my six-year-old sister, was very sick with a high fever. They told my mother, "You can stay at home and take care of your daughter."

My mother answered, "No, if my family is leaving, Teresa and I are going with them." As she wrapped Teresa in a blanket, she added, "We all want to be together. I don't want to stay here at home by myself."

All of us were too stunned to think about what to take with us. Father said, "Dress in your warmest clothes and your boots and pack whatever clothes you can't wear."

Maybe we packed some jewelry and some cooking pans and utensils. We had a two-foot-by two-foot chest, which we stuffed with extra clothes. That's about all I remember.

Mother begged, "My dough is almost risen. Let me bake my bread."

"Forget your bread dough," was the rough answer.

Two hours later, as we were loaded onto a sled, my sisters and I were crying from fear. Our dog started barking, and soon cows were mooing, pigs were oinking, and chickens and ducks were squawking. Everyone and everything was upset.

February 10, 1940, was a very cold night with so much snow that the soldiers took us on a sled to the railroad station at Zablotce. There we were the first people to be locked into a dark two-story cattle car.

The door slammed shut with a squeachunk and then another clunk. Father tried to move the door, but it wouldn't budge. "There must be a bar pulled across the door to lock us in," he guessed.

We were stuck in this inky-black metal box. Feeling our way around, we found there was nothing to sit or lie on. Metal rung steps led to a higher loft, which was outfitted with scratchy wooden benches.

An hour or two later the door opened with that squeachunk, and we had hope. My whole family rushed to the door of the boxcar. "We are being released from this dark prison. We can go home to our farm," my sister said the words we all wanted to hear.

It was not to be. We were greeted at the door by the reflection of the rising sun off the soldiers' rifles, which were pointed at us, and soon a neighboring family came tumbling through the doorway. This made us realize the Russian soldiers were still taking captives, not releasing them. Our spirits sank as six or seven more times the squeachunk announced a new family caught in our web of cold misery. As the numbers in our boxcar grew, so did our growing realization, "We are not going home."

Our greetings to each new family were, "Oh no, not you too." This wasn't just concern for our neighbors. We thought the more people who were left behind to report the abduction, the better chance we'd have of getting freed.

Among these 80 people in the cattle car with us were my father's cousin, Mary, and her parents, two brothers and one sister. Mary was about seven years older than I was at thirteen. Lottie was fifteen years old, and Lucille was eleven.

The stove in the middle of the cattle car had no coal or wood to use for fuel, and all of us were cold, but with 80 human bodies boxed in with us, getting cold was not our worst worry. It was so crowded that these people couldn't move around, and when they tried to change position, there was already another person in the new space. It was almost like the water of a bathtub which rushed in to fill the void as a bather got out.

The walls of the boxcar were a precious backrest, which not everyone had. The captives couldn't stretch out to sleep, and they nodded off only when exhaustion took their bodies. The people didn't fight with each other for the space. Everyone cooperated. Rock-hard wooden benches covered the four-foot-high top level. As children, we were small enough to crawl into these spaces, where we could at least lie down on the scratchy boards.

Some people were praying for a miracle; others cursed, "Damn the Russians all to hell." Still others moved back and forth between praying and cursing.

"The whole world will know about this kidnapping and will help us," one woman declared.

Others, thinking the United States was heaven on earth, promised, "America will come to rescue us."

Of course, later we knew that the whole world had its own problems and didn't know about our situation. All of us were crying. The soldiers told their captives, "We don't want to see your tears or hear your crying."

I can remember screaming, "I want to go home." I kicked the side of the car and banged on the door. The soldiers heard me and ignored me. Then I heard this calm voice behind me. It was my father trying to reason with me. "Stop yelling, Millie. Save your energy. You'll accomplish more if you're quiet."

For two more days, Russian soldiers kept rounding up more and more Polish Catholic people until, we assumed, all twenty-five boxcars on the train were full. The Ukrainian Polish people were not abducted, and those families lucky enough to have that ethnic connection, like a mixed marriage, were left in their homes.

When the train started moving, we kept trying to see which way we were going. The direction was east and north. This was a very bad sign.

The doors were clanged shut and the locking bar clicked from the outside, and now the doors were opened only when the soldiers fed us by throwing scraps of bread into the car. As soon as the train crossed into Russia, the soldiers reduced our food rations to just once a day for bread, and they stopped giving us soup. We were given very little water. Now we were thirstier and hungrier.

"Eat your bread in small bites and chew each piece as long as you can," Mother advised. "Convince your stomach that it is full. Otherwise the bread will be just a teaser to your taste buds."

I worried about our pets back home. I wished I could have our cat to hold and hug, but I knew our animals would be hungry if they were with us. They were better off foraging on their own.

The cattle cars were metal, but high up was a window covered with wood. The men broke a hole in the wooden part of the wall and hung a bucket on the outside to catch snow to make water for us to drink. Of course, the men covered that hole when it got colder as the train moved north.

There weren't a lot of men in the car; there were mostly women and children, and all the babies were bawling from hunger. One woman's baby was in diapers, and she was eight months pregnant. These people had more of a hardship than our family. With so much crying and moaning, the boxcar was total misery.

I heard one man swear at his God, "Where is he now? Why isn't he helping us?" Still others were saying their rosaries. The more practical men, like my father, did what they could to help our situation. They used a large bucket for a toilet and what that collected was just thrown out the broken window.

"May the wind carry this *kal* straight to the eye of the person who put us here." I don't remember who screamed that curse, but I do know that is how I was thinking.

I felt very embarrassed to do bathroom things locked up with all these people, but even in the daytime the boxcar was very dark. My sisters and I shielded each other to keep others from interrupting our privacy. There was no sanitation at all. We were dirty, smelly, cold, exhausted, weak, sick, crying and hungry, always hungry. All day and all night, we were hungry.

Inside the railroad car one screaming voice penetrated the gloom. "We were put in this burial chamber and left to die. There is no hope we will survive."

"No, this is not a tomb," others said. "Here we have air to breathe."

"Yes," the moaning lady agreed. "We can inhale the smell of the toilet bucket and the unwashed bodies. This stinks worse than my cattle yard."

"Forget that lady. Plug your ears, Millie, and try to imagine our lilac bushes," my mother suggested. "Remember the fragrances of the different flowers on our farm," she said.

I thought about our farm in late winter when the pansies began the parade of blooms. Father, a talented horticulturist, fertilized the soil with cow manure until it was loose and rich. Mother, who also liked to garden, planted flower bulbs, cuttings and seeds all around our house.

The early April spring days brought yellow daffodils and crocuses popping through, followed by fragrant hyacinths and lavender shades of iris. My mind wandered forward in time to the sweet-smelling lilac bushes and their white and purple blossoms that camouflaged the fence around our garden and orchard.

As I daydreamed my way from spring to summer, the bushes of peonies in late May showed their delicate shades of pink, white and red. My sisters and I were well acquainted with the seasonal changes because we weeded these beds. Peonies gave way to the day lilies with their tall orange blossoms.

"My favorites are the red roses because of their sweet scent," I told my make-believe sisters. "I remember Father grafted one bush with three different colors."

"I like the yellow, peach and white rose colors, too, but I hate their thorns," one of my fantasy sisters said, "The red, white and pink geraniums are just as pretty, and they don't hurt."

Another imaginary sister voted, "I'll take the perfume of the bushes of carnations with their red and pink colors."

As I reflected on our discussions while we pulled the weeds, my mind brought up the multi-colored climbing petunias, which decorated our fence.

I told my sister, "I think Mother is distracting me away from our dark prison. Her plan is working." And my daydreaming moved onward to the yellow, brown and rust of the fall mums as they completed the season's cycle.

My mind wandered to the sunflowers, which towered over us as they reached for the sun between the trees. Their big heads smiled at us as if to tease, "You like us only because you don't have to weed us."

I thought about all the neighbors with whom we had traded bulbs, seeds and cuttings, and my mind came jolting back to the reality of these same people jammed with us in our jet black jail.

My calm mother let her guard down, and we could hear her growing despair. "I can't give my family enough food, and I hate seeing my children hungry and thirsty," she moaned.

Father, who always knew a strong answer for everything, was silent and angry. He tried to keep from showing his deep depression. He tried to reassure us by saying, "Tomorrow will be better." But on each tomorrow we would be hungrier than the day before.

And over everyone's misery was the deep hopeless fear that seeped in like a fog, covering everyone. It was a fear of the unknown future. "Where are we going?" "What are we going to be forced to do?" "Will I be separated from my parents?" "Will I be abused by men?" "Will we be beaten or shot?" "Will we starve to death?" "Will all the strong men be worked to death?" "What will happen to the children then?" "We haven't seen the sun for a month. Will we ever see the sun again?"

After we traveled so far into Russia that we couldn't escape anymore, the soldiers let us outside at night so we could stretch our legs. Every interaction between the soldiers and their captives happened after dark. When they opened the door during those stops, many people took care of their private bathroom functions with the soldiers standing right there watching.

There were always two soldiers with guns pointed at us, so we couldn't go anywhere. We had nowhere to go anyway. There was no respect for human life in Russia, so it was obvious that we would be shot if we tried to escape.

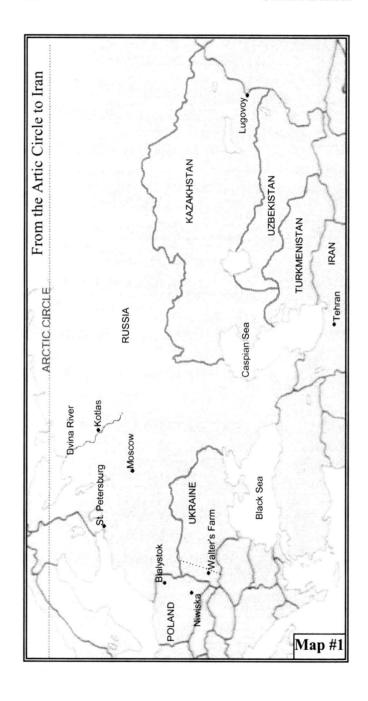

From the Artic Circle to Iran

Map #1

We moved, I think, for about a month until we came to the last town, called Kotlas, on the western edge of Siberia. Everything north of Kotlas was just tundra. We were told, "You are now in Siberia." I bitterly muttered, "Welcome to Siberia."

4

NIZHNYA STRIGA OUR NEW HOME

As we were pushed from the train onto the snowy ground, we saw a sign that read "Kotlas." We were herded farther north where we crossed the frozen Dvina River. Each family was given one small horse-drawn sled to transport their belongings. The smaller children and infants were given a ride, but everyone else walked. Teresa rode on the sled on top of our baggage.

There was heavy snow, and it was very cold—perhaps as cold as sixty degrees below zero. Our frozen feet added to our misery, and hands, faces and ears all were numb. We trudged from Kotlas for what seemed like all night—I don't know how many hours or how many miles. The darkness lasted almost 24 hours in Siberian February, and I wasn't even sure what time of day we got off the train.

We finally reached the camp, called *Nizhnya Striga*, which was to become our new home.

Everyone was assigned an area in a large barrack where they were ordered to unload their possessions.

An ugly man, who said he was our boss, told us, "This is where you live. You're going to spend the rest of your lives here. You can't go anywhere. You are slaves."

I whispered to my sister later, "His words are as ugly as he is."

The barrack was warm because there was a big stove in the center, which was already hot. Having walked for many miles through deep snow, we fell into the sleeping places we were given.

Later we learned that we were the first *eshelon* that was sent to that part of Siberia. We were the first people to exist in those barracks; nobody had lived there before. They shipped us all the way to the farthest outback. The closest *poselok* to those barracks, with a population of about 2000, was five or six miles away.

There were four barracks, and each barrack had four big halls, with about 20 families packed into each hall. Centered in each hall was the heating stove, which was also used for cooking by all 20 families. In the middle of a pine forest, there was plenty of wood which the men took turns bringing in to feed the fire. That stove needed to be tended day and night.

The soldiers and bosses came early that first morning and ordered, "You are going to work." My father was immediately sent to the forest to cut down the 60-foot pine trees. He was taught to make a cut on one side first so he could control the direction the tree would fall. He had to be careful not to knock down any other trees.

"All the rest of you, pick up a shovel and follow us," was the next order. The able-bodied women and children were given wooden shovels to clear the snow from the roads and railroad tracks. Actually a wooden shovel worked very well because the snow would not stick to it. Each day we were forced to walk to a different section of the tracks. We might walk a few blocks or a few miles to get to our jobs. I can remember being angry and cold and resentful, but I knew I had no choice if I wanted to eat.

"You will shovel until the trains can move on the tracks," the boss demanded. To other workers he said, "Get the snow off the roads so the horses can pull their sleds." These were tough jobs because sometimes the snow was five or six feet deep, and if someone fell into it, she would never get out. A few people were lost that way.

The second day we were given our permanent work. The strong men, like my father, kept their jobs in the forest felling the tall pines. Then they were forced to clean up the branches and cut the big ones into shorter lengths and load these smaller pieces onto sleds or wagons. This was all done by hand because the Russians didn't have machinery. The horses pulled the logs to the riverbank at the station, and in the spring when the ice and snow melted, the logs were pushed into the river where they floated to many locations within Russia. The wood was also shipped by train.

Walter didn't have a husky build, but he was very slim and wiry. He had worked hard from childhood, and his muscles were strong. He would do anything just to continue to live. "We must survive. We can never give up. We're not going to die here. Don't ever stop trying," he told us over and over again. Some people gave up somewhere along the way, but Father would not stop struggling. He was a stubborn fighter.

He also managed to keep up his appearance in Siberia. From Poland he brought a razor and a leather strop to sharpen it. He was clean shaven even in captivity. He would say, "A beard and moustache are too uncomfortable because they become frozen and very cold." Even when it got warmer in the summertime, Father's face was always free of whiskers.

My mother didn't work an outside job in Siberia. She was very anemic because she was bleeding from her change of life. We were all anemic, but she was much worse. She took care of my sister Teresa, washed our clothes, and cooked for us. Meal preparation was a huge job—just finding food to serve was next to impossible. Sometimes with just a little flour, she made soup so thick that we thought we were eating more.

The hall where we lived was so small that each family's space was no bigger than about 12 feet by 12 feet. There was enough room to stretch out during the day, but not so much that we could turn over at night without disturbing our family. A raised platform with straw on top was where we could sleep or sit.

The bugs also slept or sat on our straw. These bedbugs were big and dark brown, and they lived in trees and in timber under the bark. Father explained, "When the Russians built the barracks, they simply put up the wood without trimming off the bark, and that is where the bugs hide." At night when the lights went out, the bugs would come out to bite us and suck our blood.

Once my 11-year-old sister, Lucille, got a bug in her ear, and she woke up screaming, "It's eating the inside of my head. It's going to eat me up."

Although we knew about bedbugs, called *pluskwa* in Poland, we had never seen these insects in our home in Poland, but we certainly saw them now. The sheet and pillow were black with the bugs—there were so many that we couldn't begin to kill them all. Anyway, they smelled with an awful, foul odor when they were smashed. Somebody told my mother, "Boil some water and splash it on the walls." It worked. The bugs died and we knew peace for a couple of nights. Then the bugs came back as many as before. Mother did this a few times, but the bedbugs always came back. Some people wrapped newspaper around themselves, but most of us didn't have newspaper. There were close to 24 hours of darkness in Siberia in February, and of course, we didn't have electricity. The light from some candles and a kerosene lamp we brought from Poland would have kept the bugs away, but we couldn't keep the lights going all the time.

Finally my father decided, "Stephanie, it's such hard labor for you to carry, boil and splash the water, and your work doesn't last more than a few days. Let the bugs be there."

Mother gave up on the bugs, but she then worked to keep up our spirits. She told us, "We are like fledgling birds thrown from their nest who have to learn how to fly. We must figure out how to survive in this cold, frozen land."

Even in Siberia, Mother demanded, "Our place has to be clean with the beds made and the floor scrubbed." If she couldn't do that work, one of her daughters, usually Lucille, had to do it. Mother washed our clothes as often as she could, but her main jobs were feeding us and giving us pride that we were Polish.

"They are trying to make us live like animals, and we are not going to let them. Be proud you are Polish. We are strong people and we will act like the good, clean people that we are," she preached to us.

But the truth was that we were all captive slaves and couldn't leave. We were forced to do the jobs we were given. When an order was given, we had no choice but to obey. Most people had to labor beyond their physical ability. The stronger 20- or 30-year-old women were put to work in the forests right along with the men.

I worked with the weaker women, but a little later a higher-paying job opened up, so I applied for it along with a lot of other people. Latonia, my soon-to-be boss and friend, pointed to me and a 12-year-old boy, "I want you to work with me." At the time I didn't know why she picked me. I wanted that job because we got paid in food, and that meant my family would have more to eat. I was proud I could help support my family.

We were also paid the equivalent of a few cents per hour, but we needed a permission paper to buy, with our own money, any of the overpriced merchandise in their stores. After a few months,

Father bought for himself a *fufaika,* a warm coat, and a pair of *valenki,* sheep's wool felt boots with rubber soles. Over a period of time, Walter earned two pairs of *valenki,* so he kept the taller boots for himself and gave the shorter pair to me for my new night job.

Latonia, the young boy and I worked the shift from 7:00 in the evening until 7:00 in the morning. The boy was responsible for hitching up the horse and driving the sled.

My job was chopping a hole in a frozen stream and lowering a bucket down to water. I don't know what kept that water from freezing. Perhaps there was a spring there. I pulled up the water bucket and handed it to the boy, who stood on a stepladder and poured the water into a barrel on a cart, which the horse pulled over the road. Two tubes lowered over the road then spread the water over the tracks, where it froze. In that way, the horses pulling the heavy sleds loaded with logs had an easier time.

I remember telling Mother, "It takes at least 50 buckets to fill the barrel, which holds enough water to sprinkle two or three miles of tracks."

It was hard physical labor. I was a skinny, sickly-looking child in Poland, and Mother was concerned enough to take me to their physician. "Doctor, she is such a fussy eater and she won't drink milk."

"She is healthy, Mrs. Zygmunt, even though she is thin. Her body will fill out when it's ready."

The strangest thing was that I looked healthier after a year in Siberia, while everyone else lost weight.

There were other hazards with my job. If the moon was out reflecting on the snow, it would be almost as bright as daytime. On moonless nights, when our shift was over, it was so dark near the Arctic Circle in winter that the young boy and I walked back to the camp holding onto each other to keep from getting lost.

My co-worker was a considerate young man. Because my bucket-pulling job was physically harder than his job, he said, "We will trade off jobs several times each night." I was grateful to him for giving me an easier time. Bless that boy.

I came home in the morning coated with ice, looking stiff and fat like Frankenstein. Mother warned, "Be careful when you take off your clothes because they could break if they aren't partly thawed out first." Since the only coat I owned was one my father gave me when he bought his warmer Russian coat, I listened to my mother's advice.

Mother took everything I wore at night and put it into a separate room, used by the whole camp, which was kept hot and dry by a big stove. She hung up my work clothes every morning, and I wore the same things again the next evening. My boots came off easily, since they were my father's hand-me-downs and were much too big for me. I had to stuff them full of rags so I could keep them from falling off my feet. Before Father gave me his valenki boots, I wrapped my feet with rags that I coated with water, and the ice that froze in the rags made the best insulation to keep my feet warm.

Everyone was jealous of my good-paying job, because I was a young girl and I got paid like a man. Others went to the foreman and complained, "Why does she have that good job?"

The foreman's daughter, Latonia, liked me. She told her father, "I won't work if Millie can't work with me." So he let me keep that job.

I wanted that work because it paid well and I liked Latonia, and because I could sleep better during the day when the bugs were also sleeping, but it was colder being outside at night.

Lucille, my younger sister, helped our family by standing in line for hours at the camp's restaurant where we were allowed to shop, but only if we had work cards. My father and I both earned those cards.

People would get up as early as 2:00 a.m. to wait for the restaurant to open at 6:00. They stood in line, sometimes for hours, just to get one tablespoon of thin soup made from herring heads and water, nothing else. Another soup was called *owsianka,* made from water and hard-shelled oats, but it was something to eat.

Lucille was only eleven years old and short for her age, and she often crawled between the legs of the adults in order to get close to the head of the line. Most of the time this worked, but sometimes the adults yelled at her, "Get back to the end of the line." There was never enough soup for everyone. Some people got into the line too late, and they went back home empty-handed after waiting for hours.

My older sister, Lottie, was assigned work in the forest helping the men chop branches and putting them into piles. It was very hard labor, and after

three or four months, Lottie became ill and was sent
to the hospital.

5

LOTTIE IN RUSSIAN HOSPITAL

OTHER VOICES: Lottie

My name is Lottie. I am the daughter of Walter
and Stephanie Zygmunt, and Millie and Lucille's
sister. Along with my family, I was a slave in a
Russian labor camp in the early 1940's.

My job at the camp was gathering pine branches
for the bonfire, which cleaned up the forests for
replanting. This hard labor in the waist-deep snow
lasted for eight to twelve hours each day.

After a few months, I became so ill with
jaundice that I did not have the strength to go to
work. There was an infirmary at the camp where we
could go to get an excuse so we wouldn't be
penalized for missing work. The penalty was no
bread to eat, which meant everyone went to the
infirmary to get that excuse if they were really sick.

The nurse authorized, "I am sending you to a
hospital where you can get well." I wasn't allowed
to go without her written permission, and I carried
this special paper, which stated who I was and
where I was going. To get to the hospital, I walked
a few blocks to the train, which then traveled from

the camp a long way around to Kotlas, at least 50 miles away. When our family first arrived in Kotlas from Poland, we walked across the frozen river to our camp, a much shorter distance.

I rode in the caboose of the six-car train, which was used to transport wood. There were no passenger cars, and the other passengers and I sat on benches that were positioned around a stove.

"Are you going to the hospital in Kotlas?" I asked the other riders, who were Russian.

"Nyet," they replied.

"Can you tell me how to get there?"

Again they said, "Nyet."

I was disappointed by their lack of information because I didn't have directions to the hospital and I was afraid of getting lost. When I arrived in Kotlas, I got off the train and started wandering on my own. In the Ukrainian language I asked passersby, "Which way is it to the hospital?" People then pointed me in the right direction. Walking until I found the hospital, I asked for help many times because I knew I didn't have the energy to be lost.

The medical facilities in Russia were very primitive, but I received good care because I was only 15 years old. The doctors and nurses tried to help young patients, but they didn't care about anyone over 50. They kept saying, "This one is so young."

"Old people are worn out and can't produce anymore," one nurse said.

"Yes, their bodies are used up and good only for making soap," another replied.

Whether this was actually done, I didn't know. "I'm glad I'm young," I said to another patient. "I don't want to find out what they mean."

The doctors and nurses were very kind to me. They examined me every day, and I remember giving blood for tests. All the professionals were women, because the men were at the war front.

My skin was jaundiced and yellow, and I was given this diagnosis, "There is something wrong with your liver." When the doctors pressed on my liver, they could tell it was very hard like wood, and they prescribed a diet of goat's milk. I don't remember receiving any other medication, but perhaps I did. The medical staff did the best they could with the limited supplies they were given. Most of all, I probably needed a good rest.

My hospital room was in a ward with five beds. One woman patient was a Communist and the doctors were especially nice to her. She had food brought to her that the rest of us didn't have. "Would you like a piece of my orange?" she asked.

Are you blind? Can't you see I'm starving? Of course I would! No, I didn't say those rude words, which would have gotten me thrown out of the hospital for sure. Hoping she would share more food later, I said, "Yes, please. Thank you very much."

Communists were given special privileges like shopping in stores where other Russians couldn't go. They created for themselves a more privileged class of people, just the opposite of what Communism claimed to be. Their *Manifesto*, which said everyone is equal, was an empty slogan. The rulers at the top of the government owned everything; all the other Russians had nothing.

It was so cold in my wardroom that I wore all the clothing I took with me to Russia, layers and layers of it. The furnaces of the hospital were in the hallways, and I would sit with my back up to the hallway wall to absorb its warmth.

I don't think the medical staff was kind to me because my father was such a good worker and that we had some clout, but I do believe I wouldn't have been sent to the hospital at all if my family wasn't productive. Other families who didn't have workers were left alone to starve.

After a week in the hospital, I was well enough to be dismissed, and I left the same way   I arrived—I walked and took the train. When I went back to work, I was given a different job carrying tools for the laborers on the railroad, which was much easier than lifting large branches in the heavy snow.

My father and sisters also worked hard, as did my mother. I remember how she went to the small store at our camp to buy just one portion of soup, to which she added dried mushrooms and dried spinach-like weeds and a little flour, and she made us believe that we were getting a lot to eat. Mother did quite a job keeping us alive, but taking care of her family was a labor of love for her. She was a mother.

6

THE DEVIL

The head of our prison complex was a dark-skinned man known to us only as The Devil. We studied the peoples of Russia when we were in school in Poland, and we thought he looked like he was originally from Kazakhstan.

No one knew his name, and no one wanted to ask him. His face was distorted in a permanent scowl of disapproval, and when he spoke, a loud, high-pitched screech flowed from his gaunt, hollow-cheeked face. His black hair was dirty and matted and sticking out in all directions.

His body was shaped like a skinny beetle trying to walk upright but who couldn't get that high. With a rounded, stoop-shouldered back, he seemed even shorter than his five-foot height. Moving back and forth, up and down, his arms constantly pointed out what everyone did wrong.

His clothes, the same every day, were made of a dark-colored fabric covered with dirt, scraps of twigs, pine needles and who knows what else. During the winter he wore a heavy *fufaika* coat and *valenki* shoes made from sheep's wool.

The Devil's age could have been 20 or 40 or 60—he was that ugly and disheveled. So great was his aura of evil that we could sense when he was around, even if he didn't say a word.

His actions outdid his awful appearance. He was everywhere all day long, watching, spying, waiting for little mistakes to judge. We were all afraid of him; we avoided him. When he picked on people, he would scream, "Don't just stand there—get to work."

"*Kto ne rabotaet, tot ne est,*" was something he said many times in Russian. Out of his hearing, our workers mocked in Polish, "*Kto nie pracuje, ten nie je.*" In English this meant, "He who does not work, doesn't eat."

He never praised, only criticized. If I made more than my quota, he demanded even more the next time. Mean and petty, he was always checking the barracks for slackers, and he looked around corners to make sure no one was hiding there to get out of work.

The men hated him so much that one day they made the directional cut on a pine in such a way that it fell where The Devil was standing and criticizing. It gave the laborers much satisfaction when he had to scurry to get out of the way of the falling tree.

If he wanted to do so, he could get a person arrested, taken away from his family and thrown in jail. Considering the hellhole we lived in, Father said, "I can just imagine what that prison would be like."

Christmas and Easter were The Devil's favorite holidays. Knowing we were Christians, he set our quotas so high for those two days that we needed to work much longer than our usual 12 hours. All day he walked around with a smirk. He loved those holidays.

Every Wednesday night we were forced to attend a political propaganda meeting held in the *Krasnyi Ugolok* (red corner) culture center. This was a community hall with a few benches along the walls. We would all go, but my father slipped out as soon as he could. There were so many people there that he could get away with that. All the workers hated those sessions because they were too tired after laboring all day.   The evening meetings weren't so bad for me because my night work would be a little shorter.

The Devil said to us, "There is no other God besides Stalin. He is your father who takes care of you. He is the only person who can help you survive by giving you what you need. You should feel honored to be working for Stalin because Russia is the best country in the whole world. You are lucky to be in Siberia. You can't go anywhere else."

I told my sister, "I want to ask, if Russia is so wonderful, why do they have to force people at gunpoint to go there?"

"You'd better not do that," she warned.

"Of course I'm smart enough to keep my mouth shut because I don't want to get into trouble with The Devil," I answered.

At the propaganda meeting, The Devil had a record player on which he played "*Volga, Volga, Mother Volga,*" a beautiful song about the river. Another song he played was "*Nizhnya Striga,*" which was about the forest and trees of our prison camp with the same name. In this book I have written the words and the melody of this sad dirge from my memory of 68 years ago.

The Devil also tried to force us to sign a paper saying we were Communists. "If you sign this paper, we will give you more food and the best jobs. You will get more respect," The Devil promised. We were all starving, but he didn't get even one signature on his paper because each one of us was loyal to himself and to the other Polish people. We knew the Russians would use those signatures for propaganda.

We said, "We want to go back to Poland."

He spat out, "You are never going to leave."

We told him right to his face, "We are going to escape." How we were going to do that, I didn't know.

Of course, no one could say anything bad about Stalin or the Russian government. The complainer could be overheard by spies among us who could report that person, and he would be executed or put in jail. We were already in prison, but that would be a worse jail.

Every Wednesday, The Devil recited the same words, "You are lucky to be in Russia." He pushed us to be social and dance to the music. "Dance and be happy," he ordered.

My father was so happy that I overheard him pleading, "Please God, for just one day before I die, let me have enough bread to eat so that I'm not hungry."

7

MR. HARJARANOWSKY AND LATONIA

The Devil's second-in-command, Mr.Harjaranowsky, was tall and handsome, with dark hair and moustache. He wore the black uniform of the NKVD, the People's Commission for Internal Affairs, which later became the KGB. He had to make sure the slaves didn't escape and that the quota of logs got shipped each day, or he could lose his job. I got the impression he stayed only a few years in one place before he was moved to his next assignment.

Although he was with the NKVD, he was kind to us; he overlooked mistakes and didn't yell at people. "With a name like Harjaranowsky," I asked my father, "do you suppose he was originally from Poland? He does seem to sympathize with our plight. Could he have once been a slave laborer like us?"

"Don't let your imagination get you into trouble, Millie," answered Father. "He has a Russian name and he is a Russian. That's all you need to know."

Mr. Harjaranowsky probably accomplished much more with his gentle methods than the evil Devil. Although he was sympathetic, he was powerless to change much about our inhumane conditions, but he did try. Once when my hands were very cold, he called me over to his bonfire and rubbed them. None of us owned enough warm clothes to be outside for 12 hours in Siberia's winter.

My father was a foreman under Mr. Harjaranowsky, and his daughter, Latonia, was my boss. I thought she was beautiful with her dark hair and tall, slim figure. In my mind, I was matchmaking for her. From what little we saw of the other Russian men, I could not imagine any who seemed as good as her father.

Latonia had lots of energy, and she was interested in everything. While we worked our night job, she asked about our lives in Poland. I searched my memory for anecdotes from my childhood, which I embellished. Once I said, "On our farm we had geese and ducks walking around with their heads in the air like kings or queens who ruled the world. In the winter, they squawked when we, their servants, didn't feed them soon enough. During the summer the geese and ducks mingled with our neighbor's birds all the time." She laughed when I said, "We never knew whether we got the right geese back or not."

Her favorite story was about my mother working with the goose feathers.

I told Latonia, "At a certain time of the year, the geese were molting and while they were alive, we pulled out their loose feathers, which we saved. During the winter all of us separated out the soft down which was used to make pillows or warm comforters."

Continuing with my story, I said, "We hated working with those feathers because they flew all over the room. We sneezed when the down fluffs got into our ears, our mouths, and our noses. The more we sneezed, the more they flew around with minds of their own and landed wherever they pleased, most often on us. The air was so full of these pesky feathers that it looked like a snowstorm."

The separation of the feathers was such a monotonous job, but farm kids would have to help with the work at their homes. "As my sisters and I got older," I said to Latonia, "we realized Mother sold this goose down for extra family income, and then it didn't seem quite as boring."

Latonia often asked to hear this story, and I exaggerated more with each retelling. "The air got thicker and thicker until my hair was like an old lady's gray, and until I couldn't see across the room. Once everyone left the room and I didn't know they were gone for a whole hour. Another time we sneezed so hard that we blew the panes out of the windows."

We laughed a lot. Most of the time I forced myself to laugh to keep from crying. We kidded around about being hungry. I know Latonia wasn't as hungry as I was because she received her portion of food from a different store than we used. She never gave me any food at work, probably because she was forbidden to do so. Or maybe she didn't have enough to share.

It was against the rules to meet after work or at any other time, but it never came up because I didn't have the time or the energy. Latonia spoke normally when we saw each other at work, asking, "Hello, how are you?" Although she was about five years older than I was, she acted like any good girl friend.

I never saw where she lived because we weren't allowed to go to any of our boss' homes. I knew from the way she talked that her house was much bigger and better than our tiny space. Her father was an important Communist, and a person's living quarters in Russia always reflected his political rank.

My boss had no idea how people from other countries lived. She was content with what she had, perhaps because she didn't know anything different. Latonia acted like she was loyal to the Stalin regime—like she believed the Soviet propaganda. Of course, she would have to if she wanted to survive. Some Russian people didn't know anything other than Communism, and the lies were drummed into them for so long that they were brainwashed.

One propaganda claim that was true was the camp's huge steam bath. Each barrack was assigned a day of the week to use this *banya,* and everyone from our area—men, women, boys and girls, bathed together naked in the one bathtub on that night. We were not embarrassed because we couldn't see one another in the darkness and steamy mist. The

Russians splashed water on big, hot stones to make that steam.

I do have to admit—the shower flowed with hot water, and we washed our bodies and our hair with a rough gritty soap that wouldn't even make suds. We brought our own scraps of material to use as our towels. After the bath, we dressed in layers of clothes to keep from freezing when we walked home.

We were also allowed to wash our clothes in our barrack, but the water needed to be carried a long way from the well. After heating the water, Mother added the miniature bar of soap she bought at the store. She tried, but the clothes didn't get washed as often as she wanted.

8

LUCILLE'S BABYSITTING JOB

OTHER VOICES: Lucille

My name is Lucille; I am the daughter of Walter and Stephanie Zygmunt, and the 11-year-old sister of Millie and Lottie. My sisters, at 13 and 15 years of age, were old enough to have jobs that paid a few pennies and a few ounces of bread. I wished I could help my family instead of being a burden to them.

Every day I asked my mother, "What can I do to earn bread for my family?"

I was given the opportunity to help during that first spring in Siberia when my mother heard about a job babysitting for a two-year old and a four-year-old, whose Russian father and mother both worked at outside jobs.

Mother told me, "You may take the job if you wish. At least you'll get something to eat when you're babysitting."

I boarded with my new employers in their two-room house in an outpost about 15 miles from our camp. They had no running water or electricity. They used kerosene lamps. I have forgotten where I slept, perhaps on a couch. It couldn't have been too bad or I would remember.

During the day I dressed and fed the kids, and I changed the diapers on the baby. Playing with the kids, I talked to them. While they napped I was so desperate for company that I talked aloud to myself. When the exhausted parents came home from work each day, they had very few words to say to me or to each other. I was lonely for company, but especially for my family. After two weeks of boarding at their home, I longed to talk to someone besides the two toddlers.

I realized just how homesick I was when one day a letter arrived from my mother, in which she said, "Your sister Teresa is in a coma and not expected to live much longer."

I had been paid a few *kopeks*, the equivalent of some pennies. I knew I needed an excuse to get out of the house. "Is it all right if I go to the store to buy a candy bar?" I asked.

"Yes, but be back in time to put the children to bed," the lady replied.

After I bought the candy in the store, I left and just kept walking. I was very careful no one saw me slip away into the forest. After all, this was Russia, and the NKVD were watching everything and everyone. Any person traveling anywhere was supposed to carry papers stating where and why they were going. Of course, I didn't have papers, and I knew I would be in big trouble if I got caught.

All evening and through the night I trudged through the forest. This happened in June near the Arctic Circle, and the sky didn't get very dark at night unless it was raining or foggy. There were marks on some of the trees, which told me where to go, and somehow I remembered the direction back to my family. They had no resources to find me if I got lost. I needed to be observant to find my way around the woods of Siberia, or I would never be heard from again. Any paths I found in the forest did not go in a straight line, and it's possible I wandered much farther than 15 miles.

When I finally sneaked back into the prison camp at about 10:00 the next morning, my mother was very surprised to see me. She asked, "Lucille, how did you get here?"

I mumbled something about walking, but I was too tired to do anything more than fall into bed.

Waking up the following morning, I started to worry, "Will the Russian family report me for running away?" "Will I be taken to jail?" "Will I be beaten?"

If my employers wanted to punish me, they could have.

I needn't have worried, because apparently that family wanted to avoid trouble as much as I did. I never went back to my babysitting job, and no one questioned me about it.

9

MAY DAY AND SUMMER

We were in Siberia for two months when, on the first of May, the whole country of Russia celebrated their biggest holiday, May Day. We may have gotten the day off from work, but I don't remember for sure. Every one of the workers was given a voucher good for about a quarter pound of candy on that one day only. Those few sweets were a big treat for us, and we stood in line for hours to get them. True to Russian planning, there was never enough candy to trade in all the vouchers.

About this time we got a wonderful surprise from Teresa's godmother, who was with us in Siberia. She somehow had written to her sister in Poland, who sent a package with flour, sugar, pieces of bacon and barley. Teresa's godmother didn't have children of her own, and she shared some of her precious food with us. This was a huge gift, because she was also hungry herself. We were so grateful for even a half cup of flour.

Our spirits also rose a little with the coming of good weather. In May the snow melted very rapidly.

In June, July and August there were nearly 24 hours of sunshine, and no dark nights. When we planted a garden, if no one destroyed it, the vegetables grew very fast because the soil was rich and there were so many hours of sunlight. Although we were required to get permission to have a small patch of vegetables, all the families realized how important this was for their survival.

When potatoes were planted in the spring, they would be ready to harvest in September. We were not among the smart people who remembered to bring seeds from Poland, and we needed to buy the seeds for carrots and other vegetables. We traded in the village for potatoes, which my mother cut and planted with one "eye" in each hole. That one potato would become ten or twelve plants, each of which produced eight or ten potatoes.

Before we could have a garden in Siberia, we needed to clean up the area and pull out the roots of the trees to make a place to plant our vegetables. I'll never forget how much time we spent to dig up one stump. We cut out each root, after which we used a bar as a lever to pull out the stump. It was such hard labor that all the gardens were very small. This work was done after our regular jobs, because we didn't get a day off very often. People respected one another's property, and there was a spirit of cooperation between the Polish families.

These people also helped us a lot when Teresa died that first June. In Poland our little sister was diagnosed with a sickness called singa. The doctor in Poland told us, "A simple way to explain this disease is to say her body will seem to separate from her bones. Lack of vitamins makes it worse."

Of course, in Russia we didn't have vitamins to give Teresa. From the first days in Siberia, my mother and my sister Lucille took extra scarves or mittens from our chest to exchange in the village for goat's milk for Teresa. She was so sick and delicate, and she couldn't digest anything else. We sold nearly everything we owned to get goat's milk for her. I often came home from work and saw her lying in bed, and that broke my heart.

That first spring in Russia, Teresa fell into a coma. After work one day in June, Mother gave us the news we dreaded even while we wished for it. "Teresa has gone to heaven."

"I am relieved her suffering is over," I told my mother.

"Yes, Millie, you can say and think those thoughts. The important thing is to remember Teresa as the intelligent and pretty six-year-old girl she was."

Father decided, "I'll tell the camp commander."

"I have already made all the arrangements for our sweet daughter," Mother replied.

A Polish man was charged with making caskets. We brought her coffin to the barrack, dressed Teresa and gently laid her in the box. Some other men helped us carry her to a clearing where we buried her in between the stumps. Mother put her name on a wooden cross for her grave, which we sisters covered with a few flowers we found. All of this was done after work because we were not allowed to take a day off for anything, even to bury our dead. We were all so tired from working all day that we didn't have the time or energy to make as much as a simple religious service. The only ceremony was in our hearts.

And, of course, we were given no time off for mourning, and the next day all of us went back to work.

For about five weeks early in the summertime, our jobs changed. The children and young girls, including my sisters and me, picked up the thousands of branches that were pulled off the pines. The area needed to be made clean so the Russians could plant a new crop of trees. For this daylong work, we were paid a few pennies, which we used to buy an ounce or two of bread. Whoever didn't work could buy nothing.

During the summer, Lucille went off into the forest to pick blueberries, her favorite job. She followed the path toward the village to look for food. In this way, she found big blueberries growing wild on low bushes. When Lucille first brought this fruit to our home, everyone in our family was so hungry that we wolfed down most of the blueberries on the spot.

We found out the hard way – this was a big mistake – when all of us started racing for the latrines. The next time Lucille brought blueberries home, Mother said, "We will each have three berries to eat now, and I'll save the rest for later by drying them." No one needed to be convinced she was right.

I have never seen such beautiful big blueberries. The 24-hour days and the acidic soil made the plants grow huge. All summer Mother would spread the berries outside on a piece of material, which she placed in the sun to dry. She also dried weeds she found which she told us were spinach. The mushrooms couldn't be dried in the sun because they would get bugs; they had to be dried very fast in an oven. Mother fed her family through the next winter with her dried foods. We knew she was working very hard to keep all of us healthy.

Father taught us which mushrooms were poisonous and which ones were good. I think the biggest of the mushrooms were called *kozaki.* These were easy to clean, quick to cook and very tasty. We picked so many mushrooms for our big baskets that it would take a half day to clean them all. Mother fried them and we ate them like sandwiches when we had nothing else to eat. She also cooked a delicious mushroom soup.

On Sundays, if we were lucky enough to get the day off, we ran to our special place to gather mushrooms. On other days, Lucille did all the picking by herself. Whenever anyone in our camp found a place where these fungi grew, they kept it a secret from their fellow prisoners so no one else would take their precious food.

Lucille spent so much of her summertime in the forest picking mushrooms and blueberries that she was familiar with the area. Every day she wandered farther from our barrack than the day before, always keeping her bearings.

Coming home from work one day, we found a pacing Mother waiting for us. "Lucille isn't home yet. She's never been this late."

Because she shared some of her berries with others, these people now were willing to help look for her. "We will form a chain of people," Father took charge. "No one is to go outside of hearing distance from the person next to him."

The chain, with Father at the end, began walking in a circle, calling "Ho ho ho" to one another, like the Swiss yodel. With no response from Lucille, some mumbled, "We'll never find her in this huge forest."

Just as people were trying to quit the search, Father heard a faraway, "I'm here, Father."

"Come to me, Lucille," he called, and the rescue was soon completed.

"I got confused and I didn't know which way to walk," Lucille was crying. "So I just sat down."

"That was the right thing to do," he agreed.

Lucille's mushrooms were shared by all who helped find her, and we didn't have many left for ourselves. I hoped she wouldn't get lost again, because I wanted Father to keep her food for ourselves.

10

NEW FALL JOBS

In September, our jobs changed again. At first we chopped the logs that were used to run Russia's steam engines. This was a comfortable job, because if it rained or snowed, we worked inside a building so the Russians could keep their wood dry. Of course, they didn't care about their slaves getting wet or cold.

We sawed the logs into pieces, which we put into a box to be weighed, and we were paid by how much we accomplished. A lot of wood cut—earned more money—and a sorer arm. I would always get my quota of all three.

At the end of the day, a Russian man called a *dziesiatnik* counted what I sawed and recorded this amount on my record for payment. For this job we received a small square of heavy black bread each day when we showed our worker's card. Once a week, we were also paid the equivalent of a few dimes, but the store where we were ordered to shop often didn't have food to sell, or if they did, it was overpriced. All the goods for our camp were shipped from other parts of Russia, and the Communist system was not efficient.

We brought our saws to Russian men for sharpening each night. They ordered us, "Mark your saws with your names, because your pay will depend on how much wood you can cut." You can believe all of us took good care of our tools.

Another fall job we were given was cutting and stacking hay for the horses. We reported to the *dziesiatnik* in the morning and checked in with him at night. For this work we were paid by the day.

There was a period of several hours each week when we could take clothes to the village to exchange for food by knocking on doors until we found someone willing to trade. One time we got about eight pounds of potatoes that I carried on my back for the six or seven miles through the forest back to our camp. After walking about five miles, I could hardly pick up my feet, and my body felt like it weighed 200 pounds. I was so tired from hauling that *pud* of extra weight that the distance may have seemed like more than it was.

We were ordered to get written permission from the prison commander to leave the camp, and we also reported to him after we got back. There was no way to escape on our trips to the village, because we had no idea where to go. "We can pretend to be Russian because we can speak their language," I argued my escape plan with my father.

"Even the natives have to carry a written visa to ride on any transportation, or to travel outside their immediate area," Father made his argument for staying in camp. "Also, the NKVD officials check our barrack every morning."

Since we couldn't escape, the next best thing was trying not to get sick in order to survive. We were lucky that, except for Teresa, our whole family was healthy. My father worked very hard so he could get extra food for his family, and he was still strong enough to do this. He always made his quota and even more. This earned him some respect and a larger portion of precious bread, which saved our family from starvation.

We couldn't share with other people because then we would die too. Most of the Polish people were sick from exhaustion and starvation, and the local Russians couldn't help us because they were very poor and hungry also. They also knew they'd be punished for interfering with the slave system.

There were whole Polish families who were not as lucky as we were. Our neighbors in the barrack were a father and mother who were both sick and weak, and their children were too little to work. The whole family of nine people starved that first few months of winter in Siberia.

Starving is a terrible, horrible way to die.

11

LUCILLE AND THE SCHOOL BULLIES

OTHER VOICES: Lucille

During our first August in Siberia, The Devil stomped up to my father and demanded, "How old is your youngest kid?"

"Lucille is eleven."

"Her school starts at 8:00 a.m. on September 1. See that she is on time." As The Devil tromped away, he turned to add, "If she doesn't go, you will go—to jail."

In Poland I had liked school, and I hoped this one wouldn't be too bad. It turned out to be worse than bad. Only certain families with good workers were allowed to educate their children, and I learned there would be no other kids from our camp going with me. This meant I would be walking the three miles to and from school by myself.

I hated everything about the experience. We studied math, which was very hard for me. To make matters worse, the teacher spoke Russian, and Polish was my first language.

They also taught history, but it was twisted and distorted into a propaganda story. All the history I learned in Poland was now different in Siberia. The Communists said, "We were forced to defend ourselves in 1939 because Poland invaded Russia."

I knew this wasn't true because we lived right at the border when the Communist soldiers streamed into eastern Poland. We were there. When the Russians invaded our country, I knew the entire Polish army, including my father, was at the western front fighting the Germans. I wanted to tell the class the truth, but I didn't dare.

Whether the teacher was a man or a woman, I don't remember. If he or she had picked on me, I would have kept that memory forever. I soon figured out that the bullies, not the teacher, ran the school. The mean kids bullied me by throwing bread on the floor. They thought I was so hungry I would pick it up, and if I did that, they were ready to stomp on my hand. One big boy stole the cross and neck chain I brought from Poland.

I sensed that some kids sympathized with me, but they couldn't help because they weren't allowed to interfere with the Communist system. They could go to jail if they were kind to me or gave me something to eat. They knew there were government spies watching all the time who would snitch on them.

Perhaps the biggest bullies were from families whose parents were part of the secret police network. I could see that the other children also were afraid of these kids and their friends.

Each passing day seemed longer than the one before. The 3:00 dismissal time couldn't come soon enough for me, but even then the bullying didn't stop. By the end of October in Siberia, the snowbanks alongside the shoveled paths on the way home were already much taller than I was. One day the mean kids picked me up and threw me into the big snowbank. I couldn't get out by myself, and all the children ran away. If I didn't work myself out right away, I would be frozen and not found until spring. I knew this because it happened to some of our people when we first arrived in Siberia.

The bullies won. My exhausted mind surrendered. "Just relax," it said. "Your life is not worth living now, and in about five minutes it will all be over. Close your eyes and go to sleep."

But then my father's voice came back to me with the words he drummed into us over and over. He said, "We can never give up, We are not going to die. Don't stop trying—ever. We must survive."

I remembered my mother telling us every day, "You have to figure out a way to survive. Use your heads."

"I will, Mother. I'll think. Help me to use my head."

I tried facing the road and scooping at the snow in front of me and pushing it behind me between my legs like an animal burrowing a tunnel, but it was no use. The snow was packed and icy hard.

"Don't stop trying, Lucille," my father's voice echoed again.

"Think, Lucille. Look for something to help you," I heard my mother's words.

I looked up and saw a pine tree. I reached for it, but it was too far away. Finally I stretched high enough to grab a branch of the tree, all the while praying, "Don't break. Please God, don't let the branch break."

By pulling on the end of one branch, then a higher one, and yet another, I managed to get myself out of the snowbank. Once I was lying on my belly on top of the snow, I was afraid I would sink back down into its cold depths. Trying to spread out my body weight, I inched toward the path. Finally I was able to slide down the bank on my stomach, making my body like a sled, until I got back to the shoveled area.

The snowbank bullying was the last straw. I was so miserable in school because I was being picked on every day, and I just couldn't stand it any longer. I wanted to quit, but I knew the Russians told my father, "If Lucille doesn't go to school, you will go to jail."

"Please try to help me quit school, Father," I begged that night.

"If I tell The Devil you are being bullied, he'll feel like we are criticizing him, and he will not give in," he said. "We have to think of a reason he'll accept."

"I don't have shoes to wear. This could be the reason."

I outgrew and wore out the shoes I brought with me from Poland. My feet were too big for children's sizes, and the Russians wouldn't let me buy the bigger and heavier boots that the workers wore.

"Lucille can't go to school barefooted," Father pleaded with The Devil the next morning.

He guessed that the Communists didn't have enough shoes for all of their workers, and he was right. That night there was a note of satisfaction in his voice as he told me, "The Devil relented and said, 'Lucille won't have to go to school.'"

After that I didn't attend school for even one more day, and I hoped the bullies would think I died in the snowbank. I wanted them to have such a guilty conscience that they worried about my death all winter. I wanted them to suffer as I had suffered, but I'm sure this didn't happen. If they thought about me at all, they probably laughed.

Anyway, I knew I could help my family much more by staying home and out of snowbanks.

12

DEAD HORSE

The snows came again in October during our first full winter in Siberia, and we all went back to our cold-weather jobs. Everyone worked every day, but if a person ran a fever or was very sick, he or she could get an aspirin from the camp nurse, if she had some in her medicine cabinet. She didn't care about people at all, but she would write an excuse to allow someone to stay home if he was really sick. Without her written permission, if we didn't work, we were given no food.

Everyone was constantly hungry, and we were all anemic. We were too far from the river to fish, and there was no other meat. Sometime during that winter a few of our workers, who were taking the big logs by sled to the river, got so hungry that they planned to kill a beautiful young horse. This couldn't have been easy, but somehow they managed to do this by stealing a tree-cutting ax. After skinning the horse and cutting the meat off the bones, two of the men came to our barrack and whispered to my father, "We know where you can get some meat."

"You can't be serious. Where would you get meat?" Father asked.

"We killed a horse and hid the carcass in the forest shed," they replied. "You can get as much as you can carry, but you'd better do this soon because a lot of other people will be taking some too. We're going tonight, and you can come with us—we'll show you how to find the shed."

Father realized we would have to get the meat that very night before the NKVD agents discovered the horse was missing. He asked Lucille and me to go on this errand because for some reason, I had a rare night off from work. This couldn't have come at a better time because Lucille and I had sneaky work to do. In Russia we couldn't do anything bad during the day. Stealing and forbidden things always needed to be done at night.

We dressed in layers of sweaters and coats. After the whole barrack settled down into sleep, my sister and I slipped out the door. That night there was a quarter moon and the sky was partly cloudy. We stayed in the shadows listening for the sounds of others who could harm us. Having convinced ourselves that no one was there, we were able to sneak well past the buildings of *Nizhnya Striga.* We met the two men who were our guides. By candlelight these men read the trees' directional gashes that marked the paths, finding the way we needed to go. They knew we couldn't be delayed by getting lost because we needed to get back before the camp awakened the next day.

Stopping often to check for the sounds of NKVD spies as we trudged down the path, all of us were shivering with the fear of getting caught.

A hungry person will do anything to get food. He will not stop to consider the consequences of his actions. His empty stomach will overcome his terror and give him the energy to steal.

We walked in the deep snow for miles to the shed where the carcass was hidden, always watching for the NKVD. We were aware they had the power to get us jailed or killed. If they already knew about the slain horse, they could be waiting to ambush us. As we neared the shed, the two men motioned for us to stop. They circled around from the back side and waited a long time until they were sure no one was there. As they waved us in, they whispered, "No one is here. We are safe—at least for now."

With an ax, the men cut off as much meat as we could carry, and Lucille and I lugged it back to our barrack, praying we could get there before The Devil woke up for his morning patrols. Finally we were almost home.

"Oh," I heard Lucille gasp as she put down her heavy burden.

"Look," she whispered, pointing to the path at the barrack. In the near darkness we saw a figure walking alongside the barrack. It was a man—Who is he? Is he a spy with the NKVD? Will he walk this way? Should we start backing away from the barrack?

We pulled our meat off the path, brushing a covering of snow over it. Waiting and watching in the shadows to see where the man would go, we saw him move toward us. I held my breath as both of us prepared to walk backwards on the path.

Then I clamped my hand over my mouth to keep from laughing. "He's one of our Polish men. He went to the latrine," I whispered.

Lucille exhaled a long sigh of relief. We waited about 15 minutes for the man to go back inside the building and get settled into sleep before we tiptoed into our places at the barrack. We woke up Mother, and she hid the horsemeat under a bridge while Lucille and I fell into bed exhausted from our long walk.

Every morning The Devil came to check the barracks, armed with his stick to hit us if we weren't ready to go to work. That morning my father and Lottie quietly went to work as usual. I was asleep in bed because I worked a night job and The Devil knew that. Mother woke up Lucille to help clean our area as they always did. My sister, though she was dead tired, couldn't let The Devil know this, because if she didn't act as she always did, he would suspect her. We weren't sure if the authorities were aware of the missing horse by now or not.

My mother hoped The Devil would leave soon, because she couldn't start cooking the meat until he was gone for the day. She knew they would be suspicious about that horse because a healthy young animal doesn't just disappear.

After she was alone, Stephanie cooked all day because horses are strong and muscled, which makes their meat so tough that it must be simmered for 12 hours or more. That night we enjoyed a wonderful dinner with the most delicious meat we ever tasted.

My mother kept that horsemeat hidden, and she made it last a long time.

The killing was a big secret, but a lot of people found out about it. Although there were no witnesses, our workers were required to report the horse's disappearance to their bosses. There was no way for Mr. Harjaranowsky not to know what was going on, but I think he chose to ignore the incident because he felt sorry for us. The labor camp authorities never did punish anyone for what happened.

The Russians bragged, "Horses are worth more to us than people." They treated their animals better than human beings. They had so many slaves who were abducted from all over Europe, but they owned only dozens of horses, which weren't easily replaced because animals have to be bought. Slaves cost nothing.

That horse's meat helped us endure that first seven-month-long winter, and our second spring in Siberia finally arrived. Our routine all winter was work and sleep. We welcomed the warmer weather, which gave us relief from the cold and the darkness.

After May 1, 1941, the daylight hours length-
ened and our second summer in captivity passed
very much like the summer before. All too soon,
our second autumn in Siberia began in September,
and we were dreading the winter, which would
follow very soon with the first snows of October.

When we first arrived in Siberia at the end of
February in 1940, The Devil told us, "You will die
here as slave laborers because you will never get
out of Russia. There is nowhere for you to go."

At work one night in October of 1941, Latonia
quietly said to me, "I've got good news for you, but
you can't tell anyone." I listened to her unbelievable
words. "You are going to be freed. I overheard my
dad talking."

When I got home the next morning, I started
singing and laughing. My mother asked, "What's
the matter with you? Why are you so happy?" She
thought I was losing contact with reality—going
crazy.

Because I didn't want to get Latonia in trouble,
I tried to keep her secret, although I did hint about it
to my parents. I couldn't stop—the news just came
popping out of me. I swore my mother to secrecy
before I told her, "I think we're going to be freed."

Of course my parents weren't sure whether they
could believe me because I couldn't give them any
more details. Mother told me, "That's not possible.
Don't get your hopes up, Millie, or you'll be very
disappointed."

Then two days later the Communists called a
meeting in the hall for every one of the Polish
workers. The bosses said that on June 22, 1941,
Germany invaded Russia, who got worried because

the Communists knew they needed help from more allies to fight the strong Germany army. We were told about an agreement between Russia and Poland to let us go free.

Sometime before this, the British government had agreed to help establish a Polish government-in-exile in London. This Polish government wanted to get all the captive laborers in Russia freed, but Stalin demanded a huge price. That price was the Polish men. It was decided they would go into an army, which would be set up to fight alongside the British.

We were being freed so our men could be used to fight against Germany.

The Communists at *Nizhnya Striga* told us, "You can go anywhere you wish, but you have to stay in Russia so your men and boys will be available for drafting into the English army. You can't go back to Poland, because it is occupied by Germany. If you do, your men will be forced into slave labor in Germany or into their army."

At the end of the meeting, the Russian bosses gave each family a special document, which was named the *Udostowerenie* in Russian. It said we were now *tovarisch,* or equal friend. We were svobodnyi *grazhdanin*—free citizens. After 580 days of hell, we were free.

The newly released Polish people didn't waste any time celebrating their freedom. Immediately several men, who were still strong enough, met to plan our departure. "We have to get out of Siberia now, in October, before the heaviest snows come," my father said. "We'll never survive another winter."

We were freed by the alphabetical order of our last names, and it was our bad luck to be named Zygmunt. It took about a week for us to leave with the last group, and all of us continued to labor at our jobs until the last minute, because that was the only way we were going to eat.

At work the next evening after the meeting, I received an astonishing invitation from Latonia and her father, Mr. Harjaranowsky, the foreman for the whole forest. "We want you to stay with us. You can live in our house as our adopted daughter and sister," Mr. Harjaranowsky said.

"I like you because we have fun together, and I want you to stay here with me," Latonia agreed. "I'll give you a better job."

Latonia didn't have sisters or brothers, only her parents. She never talked about her mother or about any other friends she had, probably because she couldn't associate with Russians who were not her political equal. She did feel like a sister to me.

We had joked around on the job in order to make the best of a bad situation, but we never socialized after work. I think she wasn't allowed to do that, and we were also too worn out from our work. I truly liked Latonia. She was helpful to me on the job. When I dug into the ice for water, she helped me pull up the heavy bucket. I just knew she cared.

It warmed my heart to get that invitation, but I didn't even have to think about it. What I didn't say was: Absolutely not. Why would I want to stay in this hell of a place called Siberia?

I told my friend, "I like you and I appreciate your offer, but I'm going to leave with my family."

Latonia and her father understood why I couldn't stay with them.

Even before our abduction, my family was brought up to watch and protect each other. I will try to explain how close my family was. None of us could take so much as a sip of water or eat a bite of food without making sure everyone else was also taken care of. We shared everything. We always looked out for each other; we kept our eyes open to check on our sisters and parents.

My family was the only support I had in my cruel circumstances, and I knew they would take care of me if I got sick. There was no one else we could count on in the whole world besides our family. This made us all very close.

The Polish slaves were freed, but Russia now needed new captives to work their logging industry. We would later learn that the next poor wretches to be hijacked into *Nizhnya Striga* in our place were Lithuanians.

13

FREEDOM TRAIN

We packed our few belongings and, with several other families, we rode a wagon to the Dvina River. Because the water was not frozen as it had been when we arrived, we took an open barge across to the railroad station.

Each family was given a small amount of Russian money because they would have to pay for their passage on the train. Also, we would need to buy food while we traveled. We would soon learn the money didn't last nearly as long as the travel.

At the station we showed our freedom papers, but all the people in Kotlas already knew what happened. The stationmaster told us, "We will put you on the first railroad car that has room."

The first train stopping had one empty animal boxcar, but we didn't care how we rode. We were just happy to get out of Siberia and away from its cold weather. Again there were several families in our car, and again we were squeezed into a small space, but this didn't bother us as much as it had before when we were captives. The people were singing and loudly praying on rosaries to give thanks for their freedom. Although there was concern for our future, the important thing was that we were no longer slaves. We were told we must stay in Russia, and we knew we could travel east or south, but not west toward Poland because at that time, the western part of Russia was still occupied by Germany.

My father was chosen to be a leader who got off the train to receive food for our boxcar. He was told, "Give us the names of the people with you." He received so many loaves of bread, so much flour, maybe some barley, all apportioned out according to the number of people he represented. I don't remember who arranged this food distribution or how we knew about it.

Whenever our locomotive received a signal that another train was coming, the first train pulled over onto a side track and stopped. Or perhaps the engines needed to take on water or wood. I asked my mother, "Do you suppose these logs could be from the same Siberian trees my father chopped down and I cut into smaller pieces?"

The locomotive might stop for a couple of minutes or for several hours to take on cargo, or it could sit on the track for two or three days. We never knew how long the train would stay in one place. When we asked the engineer, he said, "We don't know. When we're told to leave, we go."

When our locomotive stopped, people jumped down and scrounged for wood to get a fire lit immediately. They started a campfire right there on the ground in the space of about eight feet between trains. My mother often made soup with water and flour. She needed to stay alert, because sometimes she looked up from her cooking and her boxcar was moving. Once we left a pot boiling on the fire because the locomotive started up suddenly and we had to jump on our boxcar or we would be left behind.

Often the train stopped at railroad stations with so many tracks that we couldn't even count them— more than ten or twelve—perhaps as many as four or five dozen.

One day Walter, along with our other representative, was told, "Go to the *magazin* and you will get some food for your boxcar."

When he came back to our car, the whole train was gone. He went to the station, and the first question the authorities asked was, "What is the number of your engine?" Father didn't expect to be lost, so he didn't memorize the number of the locomotive. I don't think any of us even realized the trains were numbered. If he knew that information, our boxcar would have been much easier to locate.

We could do nothing to help him find us. Now that he was gone, a new leader was chosen to go to the *magazin* to receive our portion of bread and grains.

Lugging his sack of food for the people in our boxcar, Walter jumped from one train to another, always asking, "Where do you think the refugees went? Which way did they go?" The station people told him which train to catch. He was beginning to lose hope he would ever see his family again, when, after nine days, his locomotive stopped at a station, and there we were.

When we saw him, we all jumped on him at once, hugging and kissing him. I didn't often see emotion from my father, but this time I could tell from the expression on his face that he was very happy to find his family. He told us, "I knew I could survive being separated from my family, but I was worried that my wife and children couldn't."

It was a miracle Father found us. Some of the people got lost and never did find their families. Father laughed when he said, "The only good thing about my separation is that I ate very well for those lost nine days."

We later realized the reason it was easy to get lost was because the train tracks went all over Russia's seven time zones, east and west, north and south, like a huge maze. There wasn't just one railroad going across Russia. I remember we passed Moscow four times on our trip out of Siberia. We didn't travel west of Moscow though, because of the German occupation.

We didn't see any large encampments of the Russian army, only individual soldiers. We thought they were there, but they were not close to the railroad tracks. Of course, we wouldn't see much while riding inside a boxcar, and we were always busy planning how to get more food.

Several weeks after Father was found, the allotments of food from the *magazins* ended, and we were again getting hungry with no bread to eat. When our train stopped, my girlfriend said, "Come on, Millie. Let's knock on doors and beg. I know we can get some food."

We crossed several tracks to get to a village where there were nice houses. Because it was during the war and Germany was occupying Russia, the Soviet people knew the Polish men were going to fight against Germany and they wanted to help us. They were so generous to a couple of rag-tag kids. Some would give us bread, some would give us potatoes, which was not much at all, but without this food we had nothing.

When we got back to the train after about 20 minutes, it was no longer there. It disappeared. "What are we going to do?" we asked ourselves.

"Let's go to the station and start crying," my girlfriend said. A conductor and a lady who may have been the stationmaster were at the counter. I didn't remember the number of the train either, but I did know that the last boxcar was painted white. The Stationmaster said, "Don't worry. We will help you."

Soon a passenger train came into the station, and the lady put us on a first-class car. It was occupied by Communists from the west of Russia who were being evacuated to the east out of the harm's way of the German army. These people accepted us like one of their own, trying to comfort us by saying, "We have bread and apples. Come and eat with us. Don't cry. We'll let you stay with us until you find your parents."

Their first-class passenger train was equipped with nice couches and sleeping compartments and—wonder of all wonders—bathrooms. I had never seen an indoor bathroom before, not even in a house.

At every station where the train stopped, we looked for a white caboose. I got off and screamed the names of my mother and father, and my girlfriend did the same on the other side of the car. All day we jumped down and yelled names. In the evening it got very dark, and we thought we were lost forever. "We are never going to find our families."

Meanwhile, every time my family's train stopped, my mother ran up and down between the tracks, calling my name. Late that first night we stopped at one station and I saw a train with a white caboose in the back. We now had hope. All of a sudden I heard my name. It was my mother yelling. "Millie, Millie," over and over. We were standing on the steps of the passenger car when I saw Mother hurrying toward us from far away. Comfortable couches—indoor bathrooms—I didn't care about those things. I wanted my family.

"I'm here, Mother, I'm here." I shouted as I ran to meet her. I cannot believe how good she looked to me.

In that way, my girlfriend and I found our parents and families. Then everyone was crying, laughing and hugging one another. After my family welcomed me back, they hugged my friend too, while her parents were embracing me. And yes, that was another emotional happy reunion.

After that separation, everyone in our boxcar memorized the number of our locomotive. Many times I heard someone repeating, "346—346—346."

14

KAZAKHSTAN

We were freed in early October of 1941, and we rode our boxcar all over Russia for the next two months.

Sometimes the train would stop at a station and the Russian soldiers would point at some of our people in the boxcar, "Pack up your family's belongings and get off." No one was given a choice. Wherever in Russia they happened to be at the time, they had to obey and leave their boxcar.

One day the train stopped, but before we could stir from our sprawling positions, our boxcar door slid open and a Russian soldier barked at my father, "You there, pack your stuff and get off the train."

Shoving our belongings into bundles and bags, we scurried to obey as the soldier repeated, "Get your family off the train now."

The weather was warm with a mild breeze on this December day of 1941. We saw no trees on the flat grasslands, which we learned were called *steppes*.

"Where are we?" was the first question Father, in his most polite Ukrainian language, asked the man behind the counter at the train station.

"This is the republic of Kazakhstan," the man answered.

"Where should we go now?" my father asked.
"See that wagon hitched to the pair of oxen outside? The driver is waiting for you. He'll give you a ride to a commune called Maincom. They'll give you jobs and a roof over your heads."

It was obvious to us the stationmaster and driver knew we were coming before we did, and there was no choice for us except to follow their directions, although we were uneasy.

On the way to our new home we met a Kazakh man driving another creaky cart pulled by an ox. I heard one of my sisters say these choked words: "The Devil. That man's black hair and dark complexion remind me of The Devil." She muttered the words we were all thinking.

"Don't jump to conclusions," advised Father. "He isn't The Devil, and there may not be any more people who look like him."

We bumped down the road for about six miles until we came to the buildings of Maincom, where we saw more of the short, dark-skinned Kazakhs. "We've landed in another Satan's hell," I worried aloud.

Because we had been deceived so many times by The Devil, we vowed never to trust anything these people did or said. However, we noticed none of the noisy orders, arrogant swagger or sneaky spying. We would soon find out that the Kazakhs were just as poor and oppressed as we were. They hated the Russian Communists and secret police as much as we did. This area had been occupied by the Kazakhs for centuries, but the Soviets brought in many other peoples. Someone told us there were 32 different ethnic groups in Kazakhstan. It was as if the Communists wanted to keep everyone moving around so no one group could organize against the government.

It was a lucky chance the Zygmunts landed in a southern republic named Kazakhstan, where our state-controlled collective farm, or *Kohloz*, was called Maincom. We were fortunate because this was the warmest part of Russia. Other families were not as lucky as we were.

The best part about being in the rich farming area of Kazakhstan was that we now got enough to eat, especially since my mother went to work in the vegetable garden of that commune.

My father was assigned to a job in a barn taking care of the oxen that pulled big wagons, which were loaded with vegetables like carrots, potatoes, onions and beets.

One day Lottie was standing near Father when his supervisor asked him, "Did you fight with your country's army in the Battle of Poland?"

Walter, using the fact that he was not as proficient with Russian as with Polish, stalled for a few moments while he composed his thoughts. He was proud of his service with General Haller's Blue Army and often told his family the story of that battle, but it would not be the best thing to say that here. Father looked Lottie right in the eye as if to will her to keep quiet. "Oh no," he lied. "I was too young to be in the army at that time."

"It's a good thing for you that you didn't fight with General Haller," the Russian boss growled. "I hated him and every one of his soldiers. They forced us right out of Poland. If I ever find one of those assholes, I'm going to make his life miserable."

Father didn't say anything else, and Lottie told us later, "I held my jaws clamped together so I couldn't say a word."

Because he knew the authorities were closely watching him, Father couldn't do anything suspicious like stealing food. His wagon was searched every day, and he was frisked when he left work, but Mother wasn't. She smuggled vegetables out of the garden in her underwear so we would have something to eat. She might walk away from work with potatoes under her arms, or carrots in her pocket, or beets and onions in the waistband of her underpants. It is still amazing to me that no one searched this woman with the lumpy body.

"Some of the bosses sympathize with us and want us to have that food," Father decided.

We cooked the healthiest suppers in the evening after all of us got back from work. Even after the frost, Mother figured out how to use frozen vegetables. She would pick up the frozen potatoes and make pancakes. At first, the authorities didn't care, but they made her stop taking the potatoes after they learned she was using them to feed her family.

They warned, "You are paid for your work, and you are ordered to buy your food from the government store at the commune. You're not supposed to be making your meals from produce you take from the garden at your job."

Soon the Communists began watching Mother, which was not a problem for us. What she couldn't take from her job, her three daughters stole later after dark. Again, sneaky things needed to be done at night.

Although our area of Kazakhstan experienced many freezing temperatures during the winter, there was no frost line in the ground, and root vegetables like onions, beets, potatoes and carrots could be pulled up all winter. We were eating very well.

Lottie, Lucille and I were given jobs picking cotton in the fields. To get the biggest and wettest cotton, we would sneak into the cotton fields early in the morning before the foreman came. When our dewy blossoms were weighed, they were heavier than the drier ones, and we got paid more. We knew we would have to cheat in order to survive.

One day Lucille was coming home alone from her cotton-picking job when someone started chasing her. She ran as fast as she could, and her heart started racing and pounding. My younger sister felt so ill that Mother told the camp commander, who gave permission for her to walk with Lucille to the hospital about two or three miles away.

This facility was clean and organized. Lucille got a cot to sleep on, and she was given some kind of medication. The doctors decided, "Lucille, you have suffered a heart attack." Perhaps they gave a serious diagnosis so people would think their hospital and doctors were miracle workers, but heart attack or not, three days later she was back at work.

Cotton was picked as late in the season as December, January or February. Because the socks we brought from Poland were worn out, my mother made thread from the cotton and we crocheted socks to wear on our feet. It was lucky we learned this skill in Poland.

There were people who treated us kindly. Living near us in Kazakhstan were Russians of German descent who managed the communes. They were good people who felt sorry for us, and they invited us to their houses and gave us bread, soup and vegetables like tomatoes or carrots, as well as puffy home-baked white bread which we thought was delicious.

By this time we owned so few clothes that we wrapped ourselves in a blanket while our one change of clothing was being washed and hung up to dry on a stick. When the German lady of the house heard about our lack of clothing, she proclaimed, "I'll see what I can find for you."

She gave us clean used shirts and dresses, which were much better than the worn-out rags we brought from Poland two years before. The socks she gave us fit better than the ones we crocheted, which we didn't throw away. We kept everything because we might need it later.

These German people lived in nice clean houses with two rooms, and they owned porcelain dishes for their table and lacy curtains on their windows. We were so impressed, because we hadn't seen this nice a place for a long time. My mother said, "They are the richest people we've met since leaving Poland. I'm not jealous, but we do need to get out of Russia as soon as possible so we can work ourselves into a more comfortable life."

When we first came to Kazakhstan, the commune authorities let us use a small space in a goat barn for our living quarters. This area was smaller than half of our bedroom in Poland. Only one or two people could work in the kitchen at one time. If three people were standing there, no one was able to move.

There was a stove big enough for our cooking pot in the kitchen, but we didn't have the wood to burn. I asked my family, "With all those trees we harvested in Siberia, why is it that we have no wood here?"

The answer was, "Because the Communist system doesn't work."

As my sisters and I labored in the field, we solved the fuel problem by picking up the dried cotton branches and bringing them home. We also gathered dried cow pies which, mixed with the branches, made a good fire. Because there was no wood to burn, the stove needed to be fed constantly to keep its heat long enough to cook our simple supper.

All five of us slept on a clay platform. Our sleeping area was small, and when someone turned over in his or her sleep, everyone had to turn. As rugged as our place was, we knew we were luckier than people who came later. They stayed outside, warm or cold, rain or shine, because they couldn't find indoor shelter of any kind.

After we had been in Kazakhstan for two or three months, Russia and England began organizing the Polish military units, and they drafted my father to serve in his country's army for the fourth time. We didn't know how they discovered where he was, but later we found out that in the 1940's there were well over a million NKVD agents in Russia who could easily keep track of all their own people and the Polish families too.

Walter packed his belongings and went to the railroad station. He was taken away from us to a place called Lugowoj, where he was assigned to a military unit. Father was soon in uniform and quickly trained, and he and all the other Polish refugee/soldiers now received their meals from the English government.

A few weeks later while working in the field, a friend, who was also a soldier's wife, told Mother about a letter she received from her husband. He wrote, "Come to Lugowoj now because the Polish army will be moved to the Middle East in about a week."

My father also wrote a couple of letters to us in which he told us, "Pack all our possessions and come to Lugowoj where I am. You have to take this chance now to get started on your way out of Russia or you might never get out." But Father's letters were lost, and we did not know about them until we found him again later.

My mother, as if she read Father's mind, agreed with her friend. "Let's get out. Let's get out now. This may be the only chance we have to leave this hell of a country." We trusted our mother, and my sisters and I agreed, "Yes, we want to leave Russia too."

The friend and Mother went to the commune office and begged the commander, "We are free citizens. Give us a wagon ride to the railroad station." They showed him the letter explaining where the army was.

It worked. The commander gave us transportation to the railroad. This was now in the early springtime of 1942. We asked the stationmaster to put us on any railroad car.

"The passenger cars are for the soldiers only. No boxcars have room for you. Absolutely not," was the terse answer. "Go back to the commune because we're not going to let you get on any train. They are all full."

Stephanie asserted, "I'm not going back. My husband is at Lugowoj and we are going there." The two mothers cried and begged, argued and yelled.

Crying worked. Probably because the station people were tired of listening to us, they finally backed down, "There will be a train tomorrow."

They shooed us out and locked the station for the night. As the cold wind blew, the most protected corner outside became our overnight bedroom. All of us were cocooned in together, covered with every piece of clothing or scrap of blanket we could find in our meager possessions. Maybe we napped a few moments here and there during that long night.

Morning came at last, and the train arrived at the station. There were no passenger cars, only cattle boxcars, which were already jammed with refugees. The stationmaster changed his mind, "No, you cannot get on that train."

Again Mother pleaded and cried.

"*Nyet, nyet, nyet.* Can't you see there is no room on that train?"

Mother gave up and began heating milk at a fire she built alongside the tracks. One of the refugees on the train called her over. "If you give us your milk, we will make room for you in the boxcar."

Noticing the gaunt look of the boxcar lady, my mother handed the milk to her.

As the train began to pull out of the station, Mother disobeyed the stationmaster. She shoved Lottie, Lucille and me onto the steps of the train. "Jump on. Get up there. Move," she yelled. We wanted to push our way into the boxcar itself, but Mother had other ideas. "Those people don't look healthy. They may have diseases that we don't want. Stay away from them."

As the locomotive gained speed, we stood on the steps hanging onto the railings with our cold, numb hands. We couldn't think about anything except holding onto the railing.

As the train moved faster and faster, the wind swirling by became a tempter trying to get someone to fly off with it. The ground became an invisible blur lulling our tired bodies to relax and let go. Train wheels whirling on the track beat a tantalizing rhythmic ta da dum—ta da dum—ta da dum.

Ta da come—ta da come—won't you come—won't you come—won't you come.

On the curves, centrifugal force pulled us out like a carnival merry-go-round.

I know God gave us the strength to stay on those steps, and He was helped by His agent, my mother, who begged, cajoled and threatened, "Wake up. Pay attention. Hold on or else. . . ."

We held on because we had to. If anyone fell off, she would be killed. And we held on because Mother forced all of us to stay alert while we stood on those steps.

We were able to balance ourselves by leaning into the small platform between the cars. The

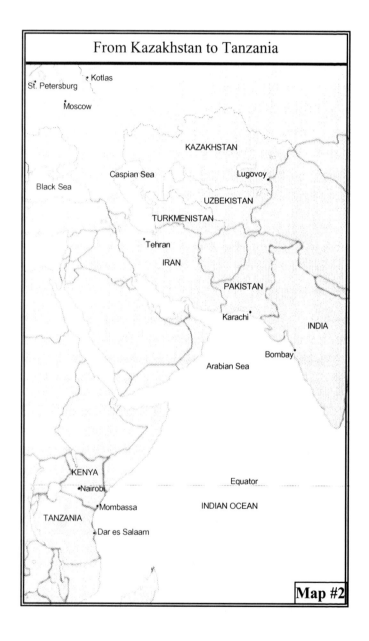

From Kazakhstan to Tanzania

Map #2

boxcar stopped at every small station, and it seemed as though we rode for days, but it was probably several hours.

Finally our family arrived at Logowoj in Kazakhstan where the Polish government was mobilizing its troops. I think this location was near the capitol city of Alma Ata. Anyway, it was where my father was, or so we thought. When we got there, we learned my father's army unit had already been shipped out to Pahlavi in Iran. Then we became afraid because there was nowhere for us to go. We planned to stay with him even while he was in the army.

Again the authorities told us, "Go back to the commune where you came from because we don't have room for any more people."

My mother looked them right in the eye and snapped, "Since you took my husband, you have to take us. You can kill us here or do anything else, but we're not going back. There is no way for us to get back there." Hopeful that we could get to a better place, we agreed with Mother's decision.

There was confusion everywhere with thousands and thousands of refugees milling around at Logowoj, and the Polish government-in-exile didn't know what to do with all those people. Each family carved out an outdoor area where they could at least be together. We had just a small place outside, but it was not too cold here because this area was in the southernmost part of the republic of Kazakhstan. By now it was the end of March in 1942.

We stayed there overnight, and the next day the Polish government-in-exile representative asked the

Russians for a train to ship us to the Caspian Sea.
They packed us into a boxcar like sardines in a can.
In spite of Mother's careful planning to keep us
away from other refugees because of diseases, she
told us, "We have no choice if we want to get out of
Russia. Get into the boxcar, but try not to let anyone
cough on you."

There were about a hundred people in that
boxcar, and we rode in a standing position for about
four days until we got to the Caspian Sea at
Krasnovodsk in Turkmenistan.

Three or four times someone, I don't know who,
gave us toast that was burnt black, but we didn't
care how charred the toast was or where it came
from. We were just grateful to have something,
anything, to chew on.

15

COUSIN MARY

My cousin, Mary, her two brothers and a sister,
and their parents were not as healthy as we were.
Both of Mary's parents and one brother were sick in
Siberia and couldn't work. If they had all been well,
they would have fared better than most families in
our camp because they were six adults with no
small children.

For part of their trip south out of Siberia, our cousins rode on a river barge, sometimes swimming alongside because they helped move the barge when it became grounded. The family members got typhoid and dysentery. Mary's parents and one brother died along the way and were buried in Russia.

Mary and her surviving brother and sister traveled for two months and ended up in Uzbekistan, a republic of Russia where the conditions were even worse than Siberia. They were forced to eat dogs and rats to survive.

Although it was a farming area and the summer weather was warm, cotton was the only crop that was raised at their commune. There were no vegetables to eat. The Communists were too uncaring, or cruel, or stupid, to also raise vegetables with which to feed their cotton workers.

By the time Mary and her brother and sister reached Uzbekistan, there were hordes of people. Those arriving later came in such swarms that they were like a river of starving humans who were flowing ahead, always scrounging for food. The local people were overwhelmed, and they turned the refugees away, giving these beggars the name of *svoloch,* human scum.

We later heard some awful stories from other survivors. In some places the Polish refugees, in order to stay alive, dug up the roots of bushes to eat for food. In other areas, they ate the bodies of people who died. Many years later Mary told us, "I don't ever want to talk about our experiences getting out of Russia—it is just too painful."

This was the same stylish, elegant cousin Mary I had idolized back in Poland.

Mary and our other cousins, about four to eight years older than we were, joined the Polish army in Russia so they would have something to eat. The army took the women too, and Mary's younger sister, who was too young for the army, signed up for the junior army. They were soon shipped out to the Middle East.

16

IRAN

In the spring of 1942, we got to the Caspian Sea at Krasnovodsk in Turkmenistan, where there were many kinds of seagoing transportation. We were put on a huge barge that took us to Pahlavi, Persia (now called Bandar-e Anzali, Iran), a journey of several hours. Because the trip was short, we weren't given anything to eat.

On this barge there were thousands and thousands of Polish civilians, former Siberian laborers, and this made for crowded conditions with many sick people. Again, my mother warned, "Stay close together and away from other refugees."

Even with all the negatives, the weather was so mild that it wasn't a bad trip. We were dropped off the barge onto a beautiful beach where the Polish army was camped on the sands in thousands of tents.

Our family was in good condition compared to most of the others. We saw kids whose arms and legs were like sticks, but their bellies were all distended and bloated from starvation. Their stomachs were like barrels, and they walked around like ghostly scarecrows. When we saw those kids, we realized we were among the luckier ones. In Kazakhstan, my mother had been a good vegetables-in-her-underwear smuggler who made sure we experienced a few months of eating good vegetables to get healthy again.

The Red Cross told us, "Take off the dirty clothes you are wearing." These rags were collected and burned by the soldiers. After our showers, we were inoculated, disinfected and fed. We were given haircuts and clean used clothes, because most everyone's old clothes had lice and infections like impetigo or ringworm.

I saw children and adults whose bodies were crawling with hundreds of lice, and all these people got their heads shaved. At that time my long braids hung down to my waist, and the authorities checked my head, but they didn't shave my hair because it was clean. There was a Polish organization, which I think was called *Urna*, that helped the Red Cross. I don't remember—perhaps the *Polski Czerwony Krzyz* was there also.

My mother made a decision. "Since Walter's army just left Russia a couple of days ago, he must still be here in Pahlavi somewhere, and I'm going to look for him. Stay where you are on the beach so I can find you again."

She started asking among the thousands of soldiers over and over again, "Have you seen Walter Zygmunt?" After about four hours, she found him!

He was sitting in his tent when a shadow fell across the entrance and when he looked up, he was shocked to see his own wife. They hugged and kissed for long minutes. When he found his voice at last, he said, "I've been so worried about my family ever since I told you goodbye weeks ago. I'm so relieved you have gotten out of hell." Then he added, "You know, there is an expression in Polish, *nieludzka ziemia,* which translates to inhuman earth. That describes Russia."

My parents came back to where we were waiting on the beach, and Father took us to his army tent. As we sat on straw mats, we received our second meal since leaving Kazakhstan in Russia. The army was already getting meals from the English government, but there was not enough food for everyone, and many of the soldiers were sharing their food with the civilians. We were too hungry, and not proud enough, to refuse to eat all of Father's rations.

The next day was Easter Sunday, and Father spent the day with us. My mother took the last good clothing she brought from Poland, my father's suit, and bartered it for eggs, dates, melons and an Iranian pastry like our pancakes. My father sat down and devoured everything—he was that hungry.

When the sun went down, he was required to go back to his unit. "I think we'll be moved within the next day or two," he told us.

We said to Father, "Good-bye until tomorrow."
However, his unit shipped out that same night.
We did not know when—or if—we would ever see
him again.

I was sorry Father was gone. At the same time, I
was very relieved someone like the Red Cross or
Urna would take care of us. The English officials
treated us like their own citizens, but they needed to
make room for more and more people arriving from
Russia. They packed as many Polish civilians as
they could into buses which we would be riding on
the Hammadan Route through the Elburz Mountains
to Tehran. All of us were eager to continue on our
journey farther away from Russia.

The roads were steep and winding, and there
were no guardrails. When I looked down, all I could
see was empty space; I couldn't see the ground. If
we saw another busload of our Polish people above
us on a hairpin curve, it was so steep that the higher
bus looked like it was straight up in the air.

The Persian drivers needed to be especially
skilled on such narrow and treacherous roads. The
buses would pass each other with just inches to
spare on all sides, sometimes getting so close to the
precipice that we said, "Their tires must barely be
touching ground."

The driver also had to maintain enough speed so
his bus could climb the next steep incline.

Those bus drivers were skillful. They were used
to those mountainous roads and knew just how to
maneuver the hills and curves.

Some people were carsick from fear and
vertigo, but all of us had no choice but to stay on
the bus and pray. After a day riding in the

mountains, we stopped overnight at a way station where we stayed in a shack and slept on straw mats. It was a lot harder getting back on the bus the next day than it was the first day. Some of the younger children were crying, "I don't want that bus."

Everyone hoped the mountains wouldn't be as steep as they were the day before, but I think they were. When we arrived in Tehran late in the afternoon, I saw crying and laughter, but most of the passengers were weak with relief.

The Polish government-in-exile sent people to greet us and to take us to big barracks that were renovated from abandoned hangars at one end of unused airport runways. We were surprised to be given the best housing we had occupied since leaving Poland, and we wanted to keep our living spaces neat and spotless at all times. We treasured those barracks. The women swept, scrubbed and cleaned until their spaces were perfect. We didn't have cleaning products like Lysol or Clorox. What we did have was time and energy, because none of us were put to work.

Right away we again received used clothes, but they were clean. Best of all, they gave us food like rice and vegetables and small portions of meat.

There was a public washroom where everyone took a shower together—men, women, and children. There were so many people and only one shower. Everyone's modesty was lost years before in Russia. Toilets were public also, with hanging straw mats to separate the stalls. Considering the number of people who arrived in Tehran, we had reasonable sanitation conditions with soap and water. All of us were responsible for cleaning up after ourselves.

We were given food to eat and a place to stay. The weather was so warm and beautiful that we enjoyed being in Tehran for about eight months.

Here I was at age 15, having traveled on horse-drawn sleds, boxcars, buses and barges, from eastern Poland to Siberia, then to Kazakhstan and Iran, and I asked Mother, "When will our journey end? And where?"

She couldn't answer my question.

17

TRAPPED BETWEEN THE BAD MEN

We were in Iran only a few days when my older sister, Lottie, became sick again. She was taken about three miles away to the tent hospital directly across the abandoned runways from our barracks. The English and Polish doctors and nurses took very good care of their many patients who came down with malnutrition type diseases like typhoid fever, pellagra, or dysentery. Lottie was so sick with typhoid fever, and with a bad infection that looked like a hole in her leg, that I didn't think she would ever be well again.

One day my younger sister, Lucille, and I got permission to visit Lottie in the hospital, where we found her delirious with a high fever. "Who are you?" she asked. She didn't know where she was, or even who she was. Her mental confusion worried us. Being concerned that our sister would die, we lost track of the time, and the sun was sinking when we started hustling down the grassy path across the unused runways.

"Make sure you're home before dark," the authorities had warned. "Although the Shah of Iran is very welcoming to his Polish guests, giving you housing and transportation, there are rumors about some outlaw Persian men who make trouble after dark."

Being young, Lucille and I didn't listen carefully enough. All the warnings came back into our thoughts as the sky grew ever darker, and we remembered the stories about Polish women being raped or killed when they went out at night. We were foreigners in a country with a different culture. We had been told, "Any women out after sundown are fair game in the minds of these troublemakers."

We walked a half mile or so, all the while talking about Lottie. At first it was just a feeling. "I think someone is following us," Lucille murmured.

"You're just imagining trouble because of all the stories," I answered, hoping I was right.

"No, there are people about a block behind us," she insisted. She was right. As we walked faster, they walked faster. Now we could count three of them. They were 50 feet from us. Very soon they were only about 20 feet behind us. Now the men were so close we could hear their breathing. We couldn't speak their language. That was not good. We were females out after dark. That was very bad.

"Run. Let's get ahead of them," I yelled to Lucille. As we raced, the men also went faster. They closed the gap again. It was now almost completely dark.

"Look—up ahead. There are shadows," Lucille noticed. "Maybe there are people up ahead who can protect us. Run. Let's catch up with them." We walked faster, then started running.

The men behind were falling away, seemingly bored with their game.

"It's working," I exclaimed. "We're outrunning our followers."

We were a half block, now a block, now two blocks ahead. We were getting away. We slowed down and began to relax. We wouldn't need the protection of the shadowy figures ahead after all. We were now walking at a slow pace, and our breathing returned to normal. We would soon be safe at home.

The shadowy images ahead were calm and didn't seem to be menacing, but we didn't want to get too close. "Let's not take any chances with these strangers," I said.

Lucille agreed, "Stay back from them."

As we got closer to the shaded outlines, we could see they were two men. Suddenly both of them turned around, blocking our way. They spaced themselves in front of us.

We moved left off the path and into the long grass. The men followed us to the longer grass. We crossed the path to the right. They shifted to our right. We again moved back to the left. It was no good. The two blockers also went to our left in front of us—now just eight or ten feet away. Looking behind for a way out, we saw the three following men were closing the space difference between us. They were only about 50 feet away. Now they were as near to us as 30 feet. We were trapped between the five men. We were cornered. Now they came closer, tightening the trap. We could hear them smacking their lips. They were snickering as they started lazily reaching out for us. "Run left. When they move left, dart back right. And then run. It's our only chance," I told Lucille.

We evaded to the left, and when the men followed, we quickly jumped to the right and ran. We ran for our lives. We raced faster than I could remember ever moving, because we heard the noise of many other feet pounding on the ground behind us. We kept going. "Faster," I gasped to Lucille.

Both of us were choking for air, but we had to keep moving. After awhile, we couldn't tell if they were still following or not. We forced our bodies not to stop. We couldn't give up.

After a mile or so, we chanced a look back and no one was there. No shadows were in sight. We were almost home—just a few blocks more.

Staggering now, walking, tripping, gasping for breath, running, dragging our bodies, we were finally home. We quickly got inside our barrack. We made it. We were safe.

Lucille and I had a quick conference. "Let's not tell Mother," we agreed. "She'll give us hell." We figured out by ourselves what we did wrong. We did learn, and we were never again so late in getting home. I think it was many years before we told Mother about our close call.

However, none of our other experiences in Iran were this scary. We were enjoying a good time in this country. If only Father were with us instead of in the army, it would be a vacation. None of the Polish people worked while we were in Iran, and we were clothed and fed. The food was not special, just soup and bread from a public kitchen outside, but of course, it tasted really good to us.

To keep anyone from eating more than his share, the efficient English official checked off each name after that person received his portion.

Some organization took us for rides on a bus to downtown Tehran or to beautiful formal gardens. The weather was so glorious that we could be outside all day. It was not like Siberia. Not at all.

18

LOTTIE IN HOSPITAL IN IRAN

OTHER VOICES: Lottie

A day or two after we arrived in Tehran, Mother's worst fear for her daughters came true when I became very sick with typhoid fever. I was brought in a truck to a tent hospital across the large airfield from the barracks where we were living. I was too delirious to remember much about this experience because typhoid fever produces a very high temperature.

With that elevated fever, a patient's hair will fall out in clumps, and the nurses shaved my head because they knew I would lose my hair anyway. When I began to get well, I needed to learn to get my balance back. I started by standing while holding onto the bed, then slowly taking one step at a time just the way a toddler learns to walk.

There were Polish and English army doctors staffing that tent hospital where I stayed for a month. At some point I got pneumonia too, because my system was so rundown that it could give no resistance to any disease to which I was exposed. With ten other patients, I was then transferred in an open truck to a special camp in the mountains that belonged to the Shah of Iran.

"We are keeping you isolated from one another so you do not pass around your many infections," our nurses informed their patients.

Living in a tent in this warm climate, I needed only one blanket at night. This was like a paradise with delightful scenery. At night I could lie on a mat and listen to irrigation water trickling down the neat rows of pomegranate trees. The food, which consisted of vegetables, fruit, milk and lamb meat, was very good.

After a month in that beautiful mountain hospital, I returned to my family at their barrack, where everyone noticed my hair grew back darker than it was before I lost it. People said to my mother, "She can't be your daughter because her hair is not blonde like you or your other daughters."

"Oh, yes, she is mine," my mother smiled. "I want her."

I was lucky I didn't become ill in Kazakhstan or en route to Iran, or I wouldn't have survived. Many people were so malnourished that they died from diseases before they got out of Russia. I told Mother, "You are a good mother because you kept your daughters well as long as you could. I would have died if I had become sick any sooner."

The Shah of Iran was very hospitable to us. The people of Iran, especially the policemen and servicemen, were also very kind to us. Our Polish refugees were given tours in the city of Tehran. Because I had been sick, I was able to visit Tehran only once. I was amazed to see an open market place with tables of heavy gold pieces, some of which were fashioned into sparkling jewelry. I said, "These gold merchants have to be very wealthy."

Tehran had huge wide streets and many amazing gardens. If there were poor people, I didn't see them. "Perhaps they are kept hidden from us," I remarked to my mother. I loved the climate and hospitality so much that I would have stayed there forever.

19

SHIPPED TO AFRICA

We arrived in Iran in the spring of 1942, and that fall the Polish government-in-exile made an agreement with the British government. We were told, "The English have prepared barracks for you in their African colonies. It will be very nice there." Who told us this, I don't remember. Then I heard these magic words: "We are organizing schools for you in Africa, including two different colleges."

School—we could go to school again! That was the most welcome news I could have heard, because I hadn't attended school since I was twelve years old three years before. I didn't care where we went as long as I could get an education. I wasn't sure I could believe all the promises, but I decided the English government hadn't betrayed us yet and they wouldn't now. If they were involved in the planning, it must be true.

Some people wanted to stay in Tehran because they loved the climate and hospitality of Iran, but we were told, "You have to leave to make room for another wave of Polish refugees from Russia."

Some of our people were wary and afraid of their future in Africa. Perhaps they suffered even more in Russia than we did. When they asked, I replied, "No, I'm not afraid to go to Africa. I trust the English government and the Red Cross to take care of us."

Again we were relocating. This time we rode south to Ahvaz, Iran, on crowded open trucks that were outfitted with benches.

Living in cold climates all of my life, I didn't realize how powerful the hot sun of southern Iran could be, and I didn't know enough to wear protection on my head. I developed a horrible headache with a case of sunstroke so severe that I spent six days in a huge tented hospital, and our family was delayed for ten days because I couldn't travel.

I liked the breakfasts, lunches and dinners at the hospital, although I don't remember what I ate. I was so impressed by the comfortable beds made up with clean white sheets, and by the Iranian doctors wearing immaculate white coats. They took my temperature several times a day and put ice on my head to lower my high fever. A new experience for me was the cuff which they used to monitor my blood pressure.

We didn't have any money at all, so I must have been a charity patient for those six days.

From Ahvaz, Iran, we traveled on a train that took us through the desert to the Arabian Sea, an arm of the Indian Ocean. There we were put on the top deck of a troop ship that carried English soldiers in the bottom decks. Escorted by submarines to protect us from German U-boat attacks, we stopped in Karachi, India (now Pakistan) for two days. "This is a roundabout way to get to Africa, but all ocean travel is carefully planned to avoid German mines and submarines," the authorities explained.

At Karachi on the Indian Ocean, we were permitted to go to the beach, where we didn't know anything about handling big ocean waves. After an hour or so, the Indian lifeguard began gesturing and yelling to us, "Get out of the water."

We didn't understand his language and we didn't obey him.

"Get out of the water," he screamed again as he grabbed my sister by her arm and pulled her out. When we figured out what he meant, we ran out of the water just in time to avoid being drowned in the high tide of the approaching storm.

After the break in Karachi, our ship again set sail, stopping off briefly in Bombay, India, but this time we weren't allowed to leave the ship. We were told, "It isn't safe because there is a war going on."

With all these stops, it took 30 days to get to Africa. On board ship, I signed up to be a scout leader, but this activity never started. The weather turned stormy, and almost everyone was so seasick from the choppy ocean waves that they couldn't eat. Perhaps because I was the only one still standing, the ship's nurse asked, "Will you help care for the sick children in the hospital?"

There was no one else who was well enough to climb the stairs to the top deck where the hospital was located. I was able to relate to the children as I took care of them, probably because I was almost as young as they were. I was only about five feet tall and fifteen years old, so I looked like a kid. I didn't feel guilty being the only healthy person because I was proud I could help with the young ones.

The part I liked best about the nursing was eating my own food and the sick childrens' food too. I ate like a starving animal that didn't know when it would get its next meal. Because I was one of the very few lucky ones who were healthy, this ocean travel was something of an adventure for me.

There was a storm with wind, rain and pitching seas. My mother and sisters were all sick in bed, and I was having a good time eating double portions of food.

20

WALTER FIGHTING IN ITALY

My Dear Walter,

We have come to the Indian Ocean, and we are being put on a ship going to Africa. We will have the top decks, and the bottom decks will be filled with English soldiers. Don't worry about us because the English submarines will protect us from German U-boat attack. We will write to you when we arrive in Africa. Take care of yourself, and remember that all of us, your three daughters and I, pray for you every day.

Your loving wife, Stephanie

Soon after he received this letter, Walter and the other Polish soldiers fighting in Italy heard this news report. "AN ENGLISH TROOP TRANSPORT SHIP SAILING FROM INDIA TO AFRICA, WHICH WAS BEING ESCORTED BY SUBMARINES, HAS BEEN SUNK BY GERMAN U-BOATS."

They knew English troops were in the bottom decks of the ship on which their families were traveling to Africa. For two months these Polish soldiers waited for the awful confirmation of the deaths of their families, clinging to the hope that there was some mistake, even while dreading the worst. Walter was afraid he had lost his wife and his three surviving daughters—his whole family—when that troop ship went down.

Meanwhile, when the Polish soldiers' wives and children got to Africa, the Red Cross talked to everyone in these military families and recorded their husbands' or fathers' names and their battalion numbers. The Red Cross sent messages from their families to these soldiers at the battle sites.

When the Red Cross letters were brought to Walter's army unit, there was the silence of many people hardly daring to breathe. Then, one after another, each soldier read his family's information. "We have arrived safely in Africa."

ARRIVED—SAFELY—SAFELY—
AFRICA—ARRIVED

As the good news sank in, the soldiers began shouting and crying and laughing and hugging one another.

The Red Cross supplied the soldiers with their families' new addresses. We were soon given Father's relieved letter.

Dear Stephanie, Lottie, Millie and Lucille,

It was the happiest day of my life when I got your letter telling me you arrived safely in Africa. Now I have something to fight for.

You see, many of us thought our families' ship was sunk by the Germans. I thank God you're all safe. Please write again soon. Your letters will keep me going.

Your loving husband and father,
Walter

21

FIRST CAMP IN TANGANYIKA

In 30 days we came to a port, Dar es Salaam, in Tanganyika (now Tanzania) in eastern Africa, and, disembarking with 400 or 500 other people, we were trucked to Camp Kondoa.

"What a beautiful place," my mother said as she looked at the mango trees loaded with red-orange, juicy fruit that we could pick and eat. "The fruit tastes as good as it smells," we all agreed.

Again we lived in barracks with 20 other families in one hall, and all of us kept our spaces clean and neat. Each person was given a single bed, nothing fancy, with a mattress stuffed full of straw or banana leaves. It was a comfortable place to sleep and live. We were content in Camp Kondoa, not overly happy, but content because we now had the basics of life

Photo #2

Camp Kondoa - 1943

East Africa

KENYA

●Nairobi

Equator

Tengeru

Arusha

●Mombassa

Kondoa●

TANZANIA
(Tanganyika

●Dar es Salaam

INDIAN OCEAN

SOUTH
AFRICA

●Durban

Map #4

22

LOTTIE GOES TO ENGLAND

OTHER VOICES: Lottie

When I got to Africa in the fall of 1942, I was too old at 18 to go to the only school at Camp Kondoa, which was a primary school, and there were no jobs for me there. I felt like I was wasting the youthful years of my life.

After I'd been in Africa for two or three months, a recruiter from the English air force came to all the camps in Africa to sign up Polish-speaking young ladies, who were at least 18 years old, to work in the military clerical offices in England. Three or four of us from Camp Kondoa joined the air force.

At this time Mother and Father were writing back and forth a couple of times a week, and my mother told my father about my opportunity to go to England. Both my parents were against my enlistment. "We shouldn't be separated any more. I'm afraid if we don't stay together, we'll never see you again," my mother reasoned.

That was a good argument, but I thought the service would be the best opportunity for me. The recruiter also explained, "The air force in England needs 80 support people for every pilot they have flying." I was needed.

About 600 young Polish women from the 22 camps in Africa were brought by truck to Camp Makindu, near Mombassa, to wait for transportation to England.

"The first rule," the camp manager emphasized, "is no one leaves the boundaries of Camp Makindu."

"Why not?" I asked.

"Because this is lion country. The male lion can run at speeds up to 50 miles per hour, but the females may be even more dangerous because they do the hunting for their prides. After they kill an antelope or a zebra, they call the males, who eat their fill while the lionesses and cubs watch. Only then are the females allowed to eat the animals they caught, and if there is enough meat left, the cubs are fed last."

"Do they eat humans?" we wanted to know.

"They will if they can't catch any other prey," was the answer.

With this picture in their minds, all of the air force recruits knew they would obey this camp rule while we waited for transportation to England.

After a few months, we boarded a merchant ship to Durban, South Africa, where we stayed until we were put on a troop ship, the *New Amsterdam*, which came from Australia. We sailed on the *New Amsterdam* with 2000 Australian troops and hundreds of Italian army POWs, who were officers in their army. I had spent 15 months in Africa, most of the time waiting for transportation to England.

On the ship, sentries were posted outside our doors at all times. Once a day we were allowed to walk on the deck for exercise, but never without our sentries guarding us so no one could mess around with us. I have to admit that some of the women had their eyes on the Australian soldiers, but we couldn't have gotten into any trouble with all these men even if we tried. I said to my cabin mates, "Whoever set up this system, separating 600 young women from the 2000 healthy servicemen, must have had experience with the hormones of youth."

There were four of us in a small cabin on the ship, and we were not allowed to have any luggage except for an army sack that looked like a bedroll. This was a good rule, because our cabin was very crowded and we were confined there most of the time.

We sailed around the Cape of Good Hope near Capetown and around Freetown, with planes escorting us for protection. With about 3000 people aboard, the ship was extremely crowded, and I was happy to arrive in Scotland ten days later.

From Scotland we were put on a train to a boot camp near Yorkshire in the eastern part of England, where we went into training. The Polish servicewomen were billeted in private homes, which were called hostels, again with four of us in one bedroom. I remember very crowded sleeping arrangements and a lot of orientation meetings.

After being hungry in Russia for so long, I liked not having to think about where my next food was coming from. As service women, we received three good meals a day. In South Africa we had been given uniforms so we would look official, but when we got to Scotland, our clothes were not suited for the cold climate of the British Isles. Here we were issued a warmer uniform and a wool coat, which we wore with a pair of heavy, sturdy shoes.

The English people we first met were very curious about our brown complexions, and they asked, "Why are all the Polish women so brown and all the Polish men so white? Are you sure you're all the same nationality?"

"The women have recently come from Africa, and the men have not been exposed to the sun in the cold climates of Russia," we explained.

It didn't take long for our tans to fade, and we again shared the same nationality with the Polish men.

23

GOOD LIFE IN AFRICA

For me, the best part about Africa was that right away we started going to the school, which included grades one through seven. Because the camp was set up by the English government, from the second grade on up we took our first English lessons in this Polish school. Although we started with simple words and sentences, I found spelling in this new language to be very difficult, because the Polish and English alphabets are different. Math was also hard for me to understand, so I went for extra tutoring after school.

We spoke Polish and Russian and beginning English in Africa. The Polish government supplied us with books in our native language.

Because we went to school for eight hours a day and six days a week, there was no time for us to work at an outside job. However, Mother again was employed in a public vegetable garden.

Her second job was caring about her daughters' education by taking an interest in our report cards. She made sure we studied and she went to the teacher if she had any questions about our work in school. Mother said, "I want you to succeed, and so does your father." She reported our progress to him, who encouraged our lessons through his letters.

On our one day off from school, we attended a little church run by an Italian priest.

The English organizers of our camp thought of our medical needs as well. Staffed by a Polish Jewish doctor, Camp Kondoa had a small hospital to serve our 400 or 500 people. It was not my plan to need this hospital, but soon after we arrived I became delirious with a high fever, sweating and chills. They carried me on a stretcher to the doctor's office, where he diagnosed, "You are suffering from malaria."

When we arrived in Africa, we were given nets, which we spread over our beds and tucked under the mattress to keep out the mosquitoes, but these insects often found a way to bite us anyway. All of us caught malaria many times. Some people were not diagnosed soon enough, and they died.

There were other tropical health hazards. The camp was only about 350 miles from the Equator, and the sun was very vicious. "You are never allowed out in the sun without a cork helmet on hot days," we were warned. And we were given the reason for this warning. "A few people ignored the helmet rule, and they got sunstroke, which made them lose their minds." I had suffered from sunstroke in Afghanistan, so I listened to and followed this advice.

Photo #3

Millie, Stephanie, Lucille

Native men prepared breakfasts, lunches and dinners for us in an immaculate communal kitchen. They served the most appetizing food we had tasted in the last three years. We ate mangos, papayas, coconuts, bananas, nectarines and oranges, along with small portions of beef or pork. Our cook's fluffy rice was so tasty that we asked for the recipe. "Just put the rice in the water and cook it," was their answer.

Because we were given the basics of life—food, lodging and education—we were content at Camp Kondoa. We also experienced things that could occur nowhere else in the world. One day we became aware of a rumbling sound as the ground began to shake. Someone screamed, "earthquake."

A loud trumpeting noise made everyone yell, "elephants," and we now saw a herd of seven or eight of these thirteen-foot giants thundering toward our banana orchard.

"Can't we stop them?" I asked my teacher.

"Oh no, no, no," she emphasized. "Elephants have the right-of-way. Any creature that weighs six and a half tons doesn't need permission to go anywhere. They don't eat meat, so they won't hurt you unless you get in their path."

We all agreed that getting in the way of the elephants was not a good idea, and we watched as these mammoth animals lumbered through our orchard, scooping up all the bananas with their long trunks. After they left, every banana was eaten, and every limb, branch and leaf was crushed flat on the ground.

Our camp workers took cuttings from the trampled trees from which to propagate new banana plants, but we were moved from Camp Kondoa before the young fruit bushes grew into maturity. At the end of 1943, after 15 months in Africa, Mother's life was turned upside down when Lucille and I were told, "You are being moved to Camp Tengeru, near the town of Arusha, so you can attend high school."

I was thrilled. At the age of sixteen, I was ready for the challenges and opportunities of a larger camp. Mother was told to stay at Camp Kondoa, and she was not too happy about the separation, but she said, "I'll have to let you go for the sake of your education."

The English told her, "You can join your daughters later as soon as we can find housing for the three of you." They hadn't gone back on their word yet, so we trusted their promise.

Again I was moved, this time with other students in an open truck. At the new Camp Tengeru, Lucille and I lived with other children and teenagers in mud brick "orphan" barracks for kids whose parents were not with them. These kids were all easy to live with, probably because their life was so good in Africa compared to Siberia. Our guardians also lived with us, and they were just as strict and loving as parents.

Camp Tengeru, home to 2000 Polish refugees, was spread out over three miles. It was set up and supervised by retired British army officers, but run by Polish citizens. All these people were very good to us; they treated us like human beings. We were given few responsibilities outside of our school-work, because all our food was provided for us, and the Red Cross gave us clothing and shoes.

"Your beds are here in this barrack," our new guardian pointed to the middle of a group of about 20 beds on wooden frames with mattresses of banana leaves. Showing us a lightweight metal suitcase, she added, "This is to store all your belongings. Keep it locked tight to protect from the termites, because they will eat anything made of wood, paper or cloth."

"These are your uniforms," our guardian explained as she gave both of us three dresses with middy collars. "The two navy outfits are for school, and the white one with the navy collar is your dress for Sunday church."

The community kitchen was outdoors, and a block away were the laundry rooms, baths, dining halls and storage buildings. The public recreation hall boasted a piano, table tennis, record player and records, radio, chess and checkers. It also housed a library, with books supplied by the English and Polish governments. The playground sported volleyball, basketball and croquet courts, as well as soccer fields, swings and slides. All these things were old, but in good condition.

I asked my guardian, "How did the British manage to ship all this equipment for 22 camps in Africa, across oceans and miles of jungle, in the middle of a world war?"

"It was something they wanted to do, so they figured out a way to do it," was her answer.

Even more amazing to me, near our Camp Tengeru, in a thickly treed jungle valley, these people built a theater open to the sky. The stage, a platform with a ceiling of green leaves and lianas, included a theater screen set up for movies, which we watched sitting on the ground. Supervised by a teacher, we marched to this theater.

The beautiful movie I'll never forget was "Gone With the Wind." Everyone loved it. That night our curfew, which was usually strict and rigid, was extended for extra hours so we could watch the end of this special long movie. On other mornings after a movie, the teachers would ask, "How late did you get home? Did you go right home?"

In the middle of the camp there was a level field where the men built a church. Its walls were about four or five feet high thickly covered with banana leaves, as well as a door and a roof, also of banana leaves. A short, handsome American priest led the mass. This man understood the awful experiences we endured as children in Siberia and he empathized with us.

Every Sunday the whole school marched to church in formation for about a mile. Because of the heat about 250 miles from the Equator, our dresses could be worn for just one day, and every girl washed her uniform that night.

In high school we were taught religion by a priest who had been tortured, either by the Russians or the Germans, who hung him up and lit a fire under him. His toes and heels were badly burnt, and he hobbled when he walked. Perhaps because he was bitter, he was so strict and demanding that when he entered a classroom, it became so quiet that we could hear the flies buzzing. All of us agreed, "Religion is our hardest subject." He taught us Latin, which I liked because I could read in Latin as well as I read in Polish. We also studied French.

Another subject we studied was English, but this language was not given any more priority than any other because no one knew we might be using it later in our lives.

To take advantage of the coolest part of the day, our school started at 7:00 in the morning and ended at 3:00 p.m. or later. When the teacher entered our schoolroom to begin the school day, we all stood and said, "Good morning, teacher," in Polish.

We took a shower in the morning because we sweated all night in the tropical heat. That meant getting up at 5:30 a.m. because the common shower was a busy place. That evening we showered again.

Our uniforms were for school or church, and we were told, "You aren't allowed to do any activity or sport until you have changed into casual shorts and shirts. You can get those from the Red Cross." Once I couldn't get my exact shoe size for tennis, and I wore shoes that were too small because I wanted to play.

The young boys could walk on all fours, hands and feet. They swung like monkeys on vines through the trees. The first time I saw this, I decided, "This is something I want to do." After the first few tentative tries, I got the hang of it, and now I traveled with the boys across streams and ravines like Tarzan. I liked this new camp because we had more friends with whom we could do all these interesting activities.

Lake Manyara was only a few blocks from our camp, and the pelicans enjoyed this water even more than we did. We loved to watch these large-billed birds swoop down and catch fish, storing them in their expanding pouch. The lake was surrounded by a fence with a gate because it was grassy on the shallow shores and very deep in the center, and we were not allowed to swim there. "You can go for a boat ride, but only if a strong swimmer is with you," was their strict rule.

And there were more opportunities for learning about Africa and its unusual animals living near

Camp Tengeru. One large-beaked bird called a saddle-billed stork had a bright yellow, black and red head with a colorful, pointy bill that was almost as long as his neck. He could be seen wading in shallow lakes.

Another stork-like bird, the marabou, was an ugly scavenger with a large craw sticking out of its long bare neck. Living in the tall grass of the jungle, they had bald heads with beaks strong enough to eat any pieces of leftover food that was around. Their metallic dark green feathers would have been beautiful if this stork wasn't always foraging for garbage.

"These scavenger birds, along with the hyenas and jackals, keep the prairie clean and stop the spread of diseases, so they are both ugly and necessary," our teacher told us.

If the snakes served a useful purpose, I didn't know what it was. "When these reptiles get too close to us, we have to smoke them out of their holes," I was told. "We start by building a fire, and then a hose is put into their hiding places, through which smoke is pumped. If all goes well, the snakes leave the hole by another way."

"What happens if all doesn't go well?" I asked.

"Then you must be prepared."

"Prepared?"

"To run like hell to stay ahead of the snake."

Once the native men caught a 15-foot cobra near our barracks. It was beautiful, but so poisonous that we were told, "If they spit, their venom can kill you. When they are excited, the skin in their neck expands into a hood. You don't want to be around when that happens. They are not nice."

Also not so nice were the mosquitoes, which were always ready to sting to get someone's blood. They carried malaria, which was fatal if not treated in time.

Ugliest of all were the termites with their fat, soft, white bellies. The teachers explained, "These insects build their castles as high as 18 feet, and the only way to get rid of these pests is to dig out the queen and kill her. This is not a job we are able to do. We hire professionals. The castles must be destroyed because an army of termites can eat a whole house in a single day. They will eat anything except rock or metal."

The weather was sometimes ugly also. I remember the roofs of the barracks were made of palm leaves and elephant grass and there were wide eaves resting on poles rising from the walls. Perhaps twice a week during the hottest seasons, the windy storms came and blew sand in between the roof and the walls. Wind tunnels shaped like small tornados covered our whole living space with gritty dirt three or four inches deep. We learned to take the advice of our teachers. "Cover your beds with mosquito netting. You can then shake the sand off your beds when the storm is over."

Although Mother also endured these same weather conditions, we described them in letters to her during our eight-month separation, and she wrote back to us every day. "I'm lonely for my husband, and I'm impatient to be moved to Camp Tengeru to be with my daughters."

We were very busy, but we missed her also. She wrote, "Be sure you go to school every day." "Are you studying?" "What grades did you get?"

She was interested in all our activities. "Did you like the play?" "How did you do on your test?" "Do you need anything?" "Do you look presentable when you go to church and school?"

She reported on our progress to Father when she wrote to him in Italy two or three times a week. At least once a week he wrote back and sent a shilling or two, equal to about a dime or a quarter, for us to spend on candy or whatever we wanted. He sent as much as he could spare. At Christmastime he sent an extra one or two shillings. That was a lot of money to us.

24

LOTTIE IN THE AIR FORCE

OTHER VOICES: Lottie

With 600 other young Polish women then living in African camps, I signed up for the Royal Air Force in 1942. We sailed on a troop ship to the colder climate of Scotland, and from there we boarded a train to England.

In Yorkshire our physical conditioning began in earnest. We trained for about a month and then we were sent to Wilmslow, near Manchester, to a regular boot camp where we were assigned a serial number.

The air force was very regimented. We were rousted out of bed at 6:00 in the morning, and lights out was at 9:00 at night. They taught us how to make military style beds. Our hair was cut above the collar of our shirt, which was no problem because the military barbers knew the regulation length. Every night we were required to polish the buttons on our uniform and shine our shoes to prepare for inspection the next morning.

We were all given extra jobs. One of mine was cleaning the living room and office for a corporal, a woman from Canada. England was so full of international military personnel and equipment that it's a wonder it didn't sink into the ocean.

English men trained us. They were thorough, but they were not mean or rough. Some of the women fainted from the strenuous marching with our arms held high, but I don't believe the training was too rugged. Perhaps these women were still weak from Russia. One of our supervisors guessed, "Maybe they partied too much last night."

We took classes for eight hours a day, learning military procedures and English. There were tests at the end of boot camp so they could assign us to jobs for which we were qualified.

My English instructor wasn't pleased when I was transferred to another assignment. He complimented, "You are learning English exceptionally well."

"Is there any way that you can stop my transfer?" I asked.

"No, there's nothing I can do. The men in command make those decisions," he replied.

When I received notice of the transfer, I was given one hour to be at the guard station with my duffel bag packed. With several of my fellow air force women, on a dark night I was soon riding down the street in a military truck with no headlights because of the blackout.

"How can the driver see the road and the other traffic?" we asked.

"They're used to driving at night, and they're familiar with the road. Don't worry. We'll get you to your new station in one piece." I decided to trust their word, and we arrived safely as they had promised.

On this new assignment, for six months I did paper work in an office in the maintenance section of a camp in Farthingworth, where the bombers were maintained. Here we lived in Quonset huts, metal buildings with a stove in the middle. We were out of the elements, but wood was hard to get, and we were never warm enough. A cot, two blankets and a pillow, as well as two uniforms and two pairs of shoes, were our only possessions. We were too young to worry about tomorrow, only today.

As meager as our accommodations were, we knew we were better off than many British civilians, especially those living in the cities. We were given three good meals a day. All the citizens' food was rationed, and they couldn't buy bread, eggs, butter or fruit without using a ration coupon. Their weekly allotment of meat was enough for one normal serving, and every civilian received just one or two eggs a week. If the English people had any extra food, like an orange, they would give it to a soldier or an airman. All the country's resources went to the military first.

Day and night, London was bombed by German V-2 rockets, which were launched from the continent, probably from occupied Netherlands. When the air raid sirens went off, everyone ran into the subway tunnels for shelter. Some people slept in the underground stations every night.

Other workers lived underground at war rooms for four or five years, never seeing the outside world. This was the intelligence room where a lot of information about the movement of the German army was being assembled.

The Allies made it impossible for Germany to gather intelligence from our side. All of us had to be careful what we said or wrote in letters, which were censored. When I corresponded with my family in Africa, I couldn't even tell them where I was stationed or the work I was doing. I wasn't allowed to say anything about the living conditions anywhere in England. About all I could say was, "I am healthy and happy." I could tell my family if I went to the movies, but not much else.

More than the rest of Britain, London suffered when whole sections of the city were bombed flat. When their houses were leveled, the newly homeless people were taken in by their neighbors. To keep up the morale of the English people, the rubble was immediately cleaned up so the citizens wouldn't have to look at it.

Parents also sacrificed by sending their children to Canada, Australia, or New Zealand to keep them safe until the end of the war. All of us in the air force were working under harsh conditions, but not nearly as bad as the English citizens.

Before long I was transferred again to a training school for new pilots at Hucknall, near Nottingham, where I spent six weeks taking a course to learn how to issue uniforms, shoes, underwear, etc.

There were three of us learning this new job. First we were required to make sure the person really had worn out his shoes or uniform. We decided whether these items could be sent out for repair or whether to exchange them for new ones. Only then could we sign a voucher; we handled no money. Everything was very controlled so no one could cheat the English government by sending in a fake number. Someone from the Accounting Department came and checked the ledger figures all the time.

After our course, we were sent to a Camp Camerigan, near Lincolnshire. The facilities at this military center were so spread out that we were issued a bicycle to get from our sleeping quarters to the cafeteria and to our jobs. All these buildings were a mile or two away from the others. It was flat terrain, but the weather was very windy. Everyone rode a bicycle, and there was a special section where we could get new tires or brakes or whatever we needed to maintain this transportation.

Three of us lived in one room in this camp. There was domestic night once a week, when we were not allowed to go out anywhere. We were required to stay home and clean our clothes and our apartment. A few of the women went out to the movies or the bars on most nights, and they squawked when they couldn't go out on domestic night too. I think the close living quarters were more difficult to endure for some of my fellow air force women than for others.

Every year we were given a furlough, which we spent with English families who welcomed any service person into their home. During those vacations, I observed their attitude firsthand. I never heard even one complaint from the British civilians. Even when someone they loved was killed, they never aired their grief in public. Nothing was published about who was killed, and only the families knew about their loss. At air force headquarters, only the number of the plane that crashed was posted, never the pilot's name too. The idea was to keep up the morale of the people by not focusing on casualties.

Families were so disciplined and patriotic, and they accepted anything that happened. The civilians sacrificed a lot. I remember once when a crippled plane crashed trying to land at our airport and citizens on the ground were killed, people said, "Thank God the pilot survived." They were so grateful to their service men and women.

They were going to win this war no matter how many people were killed or how long it took. Hitler thought he could demoralize the British. He was a fool. The will of the English people wouldn't be broken in a hundred years—not even a thousand years. This island couldn't be conquered.

25

MOTHER TO NEW CAMP

The English government had promised my mother, "We will reunite you with Millie and Lucille as soon as we have a place for all three of you at Camp Tengeru." They organized our food, clothing, housing, education and recreation so well that we never questioned their decisions.

Stephanie, my mother, was moved to our new Camp Tengeru sometime in the summer of 1944. With Lucille and me, she then lived in a small round building, shaped like a beehive, called a *ule,* which had earthen floors covered with grass. There were four beds and a window, which we couldn't open for fresh air because of the mosquitoes, unless it was covered with the mosquito netting from our beds.

Our beehive house was built on a small hill, with our outside kitchen area below the house. Since Mother came to live with us in our own home, we no longer got three meals a day cooked for us. We now needed a stove, so we built an outdoor barbecue pit using two big rocks with a stick across the top from which to hang a pot.

I can remember stirring the food in our pan when the stick broke and fed our whole meal to the greedy fire. Mother said, "Start over with a new branch and a new supper, or there will be no food tonight." After that, all of us paid more attention to the condition of the stick hanging over our barbecue.

Because we had no oven for baking, the English government supplied us with cakes and tasty rye bread. Often our sandwiches were bread and butter and onion slices. We went to a public place where the workers would ask, "How many adults are in your family? How many children?" Then we would receive our allotment of powdered milk, sugar, flour, barley and potatoes. No one had refrigeration so all this food needed to be dried and not perishable.

There were twelve sections in the camp. After my mother came, we lived in Section Six, which was less than a mile from our school. We shared the textbooks with the other students, and the kids closest to the school used these books first, a definite advantage. We studied in the shade of the trees, and after we were finished with the lesson, the book would be walked to the next student and on to the next, until all of us learned the assignment. This arrangement worked because we didn't have the same subject every day. Everyone was responsible about passing the textbook along quickly.

When we were freed from Siberia in 1941, we lost track of cousin Mary and her brother and sister, until my father met them by chance when they were all in the Polish army in the Middle East. He gave them our address, and Mary wrote to us. When I wrote back to her, I described our living arrangements. I also mentioned, "Our school is short of Polish reference books like dictionaries."

Mary was going to school while she was in the army, and they were well supplied with Polish-language books. She was able to send Polish school books to us in Africa, which proved to be helpful to the whole camp.

When we weren't in school, we had work to do. Almost every day, we walked to a stream about a mile away to wash our clothes, or we could bring the water to our house and clean the laundry there. We soon figured out, "If we carry two buckets of water for a mile, we'll be stopping all the time to rest. It's easier to bring the clothes to the river."

We lived about 20 miles from Mt. Kilimanjaro, which was snow-capped all year round even though it was in equatorial Africa. The source of the stream came from the melting snow of the mountains, and we washed our laundry in this cold water. It was a pleasure to wade in that small river during the heat of the summer. We would beat the clothes on the rocks to wash them with the soap we were given, and then wring them out. After carrying this wet laundry up the steep bank and all the way home, we hung it on a clothesline, and it would dry in less than a half hour. During the hottest months the wind came up a couple of times a week and blew sand on the clothes.

"Back to the stream?" Lucille asked.

"Back to the stream," I nodded.

"Rinsing the clothes again is not fun," we agreed, but we did it anyway.

During the rainy season this stream became a raging torrent, almost flooding as high as our homes. No laundry got washed in that dangerous river until the water level went down.

We arrived in Africa in late 1942, and we moved to the second camp sometime during the fall of 1943. My mother joined us at Camp Tengeru in the early summer of 1944. Sometime in later 1944 or early 1945, soon after Stephanie moved to our second camp in Africa, the Red Cross came around to all the Polish refuges saying, "Give us the names of any relatives you have in any country around the world." They explained, "We are trying to move anyone we can to any stable place in the world."

My mother said, "I have a sister, Appolonia Bury, in Hammond, Indiana and two brothers, Stanley and Ignatc Majka, in Chicago."

Stephanie hadn't seen her siblings since 1918 and 1920, and hadn't corresponded with them since about 1932; she didn't even have an address for them. She told the Red Cross about her sister and brothers, and she gave them her maiden name, but she didn't think anything would come of it.

I was so busy and happy in Africa at this time that I didn't even want to think about America.

26

IGNATC, STANLEY AND APPOLONIA IN AMERICA

In Chicago, Illinois, USA, my Uncle Ignatc Majka was sick in bed one Sunday morning in 1945, listening to a Polish language radio program. The rest of his family went to church. He was jolted to attention when he heard the name Stephanie Majka Zygmunt mentioned on the radio. When his family came home, he told them the amazing news. "My sister, Stephanie, and two of her daughters, Millie and Lucille, are alive and living in Africa," he exclaimed.

The first question his family asked was, "What is she doing in Africa?"

He called his brother, Stanley, who also lived in Chicago, and again he heard, "What is she doing in Africa?"

He called his sister, Appolonia, in Hammond, Indiana, to tell her the good news.

"What is she doing in Africa?" came the familiar question.

The two brothers and one sister called the Red Cross telephone number, and they got all the information about us, including our address in Africa, and Appolonia wrote to us. We were the envy of our camp neighborhood when she sent us a package with clothes.

Too small, too big, too hot—most of the clothes didn't work for us. She sent shoes that we couldn't wear, but we didn't care. We received a package from America, and more importantly, we made a connection. We gave the clothes and shoes that didn't fit to the Red Cross for other people to use.

Sometime after that, my Aunt Appolonia asked in her letter, "Would you like to come to America?"

We assumed we might be going to England after the war if we couldn't go back to Poland. Since Mother didn't know her siblings' addresses, none of us even considered America, which seemed like such an impossible dream that couldn't happen to us. At that point we didn't know about our farm in Poland and whether we could go back there. But then we reasoned, "There is no free Poland, We can never go back as long as the Russians are there." So we decided to accept Appolonia's invitation to come to the United States.

My aunt had a son-in-law named George Cvitcovich, who was a popular local politician in Hammond, and she asked for his help to get visas for us to go to America. He said he would do anything to help, but he wasn't going to support us. "Appolonia, you'll have to sponsor them and support them until they find jobs; that is your responsibility," he warned my aunt.

George went to Indiana Congressman Meden, who got visas to America for Mother, Lucille and me. These visas were not easy to get because at that time the United States enforced a quota on the number of immigrants they would accept from any one country, and the Polish allotment was not high. Also, because there was still a war going on, it was impossible to schedule transportation. There wasn't even one place on any ocean liner. The ships that did sail were used for the transport of troops and war supplies. Even after the war ended, the available transportation was used to bring the millions of servicemen back to their homes.

We would have to be patient; we would have to wait our turn to go to America. We didn't worry about it too much because we were busy with activities and work.

27

MASAI WARRIORS

And so we went on with our lives in Africa. We sang in a choir, and we belonged to scouts. *Sodalicja,* a Polish religious organization for young girls that required its members to be good Catholics, taught us how to behave. We attended meetings led by a priest, and we acted in religious plays organized on a stage in the hall.

On weekends we danced at that meeting room. There were many good reasons why this wasn't fun. I wasn't very good. There weren't enough boys, so the girls would have to partner together. It was too hot to exercise holding onto another sweating person.

In spite of all the negatives, I loved the dances. The thick walls of the dance hall were made with mud which acted as insulation to keep the building a little cooler than the outdoors. At 8:45 p.m. everyone stopped all activity and hurried home before the 9:00 curfew.

As we walked home from the dances, we were entertained by the jungle sounds of birds, cawing and screeching. The spotted hyenas hunted at night, usually in packs, and we could sometimes hear them laughing, "Ha ha ha, ha ha."

"They are laughing at us," Lucille said.

When the animals and birds became quiet, we could hear the water tumbling over the rocks in the swift stream that made its way to us from the mountains.

At Christmastime in our camp near the Equator, it was so hot that the air was shimmering. In January and February, and July and August, the hottest months, we were given vacations from school, and we went camping for two or three weeks, living in tents on a plateau near Mount Meru, about 30 miles from Camp Tengeru. In the morning the air was so clear that we could see the snow on top of Mount Kilimanjaro. The camp was set up close to a stream so we had access to water.

"Here," we were told, "you will get a first-hand lesson in zoology."

We saw a lot of different kinds of monkeys. Because they were not dangerous unless provoked, we watched them at close range. I was fascinated by the cute young ones who were so protected by their mothers that when one nest got full of fleas, the monkey mamas built clean new nests for their babies.

Lucille said, "I like the lustrous-eyed gazelles because they are so swift and graceful."

Especially interesting to me were the giraffes when they ran in smooth, graceful leaps. Eating the upward-growing leaves of the acacia tree, these tall animals could reach around the thorns with their flexible tongues. On the under side of the spiny branches, the masked weaverbird built its nest protected from the giraffes by the thorny branches.

Another favorite of mine was the secretary bird, which stood about four feet tall. When it ran, it seemed to me that its long tail feathers would propel this bird forward with each leap.

The 300-pound ostriches were so awkward they couldn't fly, but they were swift racers on their two-toed legs. "Ostriches are the fastest runners," all of us agreed, "but the most beautiful birds of all are the flocks of pink flamingos." With their long legs and neck, I imagined these graceful birds teaching a posture class.

While we were on our camping trip, the English authorities came weekly to bring our food supplies, which we needed to guard so the hyenas didn't steal them from our tent. I wondered, "How do these thieving animals know where the bread, cookies, vegetables, and other goodies are hidden?"

"They can smell the food," came the answer.

There were many more animals. I didn't like the hyenas, while Lucille decided, "I think the gorillas and jackals are even more ugly."

The camping trip was fun, but we had other activities organized for us. For three days at Easter time, some of us stood at attention for a whole hour's shift, as if we were sentries at the sepulcher which represented Jesus' grave. It was my pleasure to do that, because not everyone was strong enough to stand still that long.

One other adventurous thing we did was to go for a ten-mile walk in the jungle, carrying a backpack. While we were in school and camp activities, my mother kept busy with plans of her own. Even though she was an accomplished cook, she went to classes to learn homemaking skills like sewing, cooking and baking. With other mothers, she belonged to an organization at which they learned parenting skills. I think Mother enjoyed the socializing more than the lessons. I told her, "You're such a good mother and homemaker. You should be teaching those classes."

During the day she worked for as long as twelve hours a day in the gardens of Camp Tengeru. She tended tomatoes, potatoes, onions, and broccoli. The tomatoes needed to have soil mounded around them so these plants would develop more roots. The vegetables were watered all year round because it rained just twice a year, and at those times it poured for two days until small streams would turn into big rivers.

Though she worked hard, Mother was careful about her appearance. She also made sure we lived up to her standards of neat, clean clothes and hair. She pressed our uniforms, using an iron that was heated on a rock at our stove. The ribbons on the uniforms had to be perfectly smooth or they wouldn't pass Mother's inspection.

"Is your hair neatly combed? Show me your nails. Are they clean?" and only then, "OK, you can go now."

Even our hut didn't escape from Mother's routine. She made sure it was swept clean and kept orderly. She said, "This is our proud Polish culture."

Mother got paid for her work in the gardens; Father also sent us a little money from his bi-monthly paycheck as a soldier, and we bought candy or cookies at a little local store. Living in an English colony, we used their currency.

Father wrote, "*Thank you for sending your picture. I was so proud when I saw how nice you look.*"

I didn't have special boyfriends in high school because there were so few young men. I didn't even know what teenage boys and girls did together that caused so much excitement. I had a crush on a young man in Africa who was the same age as I was. He knew the percentages were in his favor, and he took full advantage by having a different girlfriend every week. These were our teen years, and there was some kissing behind the barracks, but no girls got into trouble with pregnancies. The camp was very strict.

After school or on weekends we played tennis or volleyball, making arrangements ahead of time because some students lived farther away, and of course, we didn't have cars. There was so much going on that none of us had trouble staying active and having a good time.

Not everything we did was fun, and especially bad were the pills to prevent malaria that we needed to take. I think the white ones were called Tobrana and the yellow ones were called Chinina. They were so bitter that the acrid taste would remain in the mouth for a week. To repel the mosquitoes, we also were given a salve that smelled like something spoiled. When we were first given the salve, I opened the jar and announced, "Yech, I don't want to use it." Then I thought about being sick with malaria again, and I changed my mind. Maybe that's another reason why we didn't date in Africa. We all just smelled too bad.

Every part of our lives was organized. For our own protection, we needed to get permission to leave Camp Tengeru on day trips. The camp authorities gave us a pass to go by truck to the stores that were owned by Indian people in Arusha, the closest big town from our home. Sometimes we bought fabric, which we took to a dressmaker to be made into clothes.

I had problems with my front teeth, and along with other people, I often rode that truck to see a dentist. At my first appointment, I was told, "You have a cavity."

Three months later the dentist decided, "Today I'll drill the tooth and put in a temporary filling."

At the next visit 90 days later, my tooth was filled. Three months after that, the dentist checked his work and said, "The tooth is fixed." Then he found a new cavity, and we were off for another year of dental appointments.

We also had medical care. When a person became ill, someone would have to walk to the main office one or two miles away. The office secretary then called for an ambulance to take the sick person to the hospital.

A native Swahili man drove the car that served as an ambulance. He was so intelligent that he learned fluent Polish within one year. We had fun with him; we joked with him. He would say, "Don't talk about me because I can understand everything you are saying."

Because we communicated with Africans like our driver, we learned some Swahili.

The natives told us about the king of beasts, or *simba* in Swahili. "The female lions do the hunting, but as soon as the lionesses bring down their prey, they are chased away by the males, who eat as much as they want first. It's a good plan, don't you think?"

"No, we don't think so."

The Swahili Tribe inhabited the coastal regions near the Indian Ocean in Kenya and Tanganyika. Many from this culture were Islamic, but our driver was studying in a seminary to become a Catholic priest.

Another African tribe living near Camp Tengeru in Tanganyika was the Masai, a proud and independent people who believed themselves to be God's chosen people. They did not cultivate the soil, but instead they lived off the blood, milk and meat of their cattle, sheep and goats.

The women of the Masai tribes took care of the homes and the children. The young men traveled great distances to find grazing lands for their cattle, which represented power for them. The various Masai groups stole animals back and forth from one another.

Because lions attacked their cattle, this king of beast was a threat to the tribe's livelihood. A Masai man needed to prove his manhood by killing a lion before his people would call him a warrior.

After we moved into our beehive *Ule* with our mother, on weekends Lucille and I went back to visit our high school friends in the orphan part of the camp where they played music and records for dancing. One time we forgot about the time, and it was soon past our 9:00 p.m. curfew when we were expected to be inside our house and nowhere else. It was nearly 10:00 on a dark night by the time I started walking back to our home with my sister. Instead of staying on the main road, Lucille and I decided, "Let's take the shortcut path through that field of tall corn."

We were hurrying down the path when suddenly I could feel something sharp being run down my back. At first I didn't know what it was, but as I turned around, I looked two feet straight up at a skyscraper of a dark man carrying a javelin and the long knife he had run down my back. Then we saw a second tall Masai warrior, and we did not know if there were even more men hiding in the cornfield. My brain stood frozen in fright. It may have been an hour, a minute, or a second before I could move.

Without thinking, I grabbed the first man by his animal skin vest and pushed on his greased body so hard that he fell backward. He appeared to be stunned when this puny little girl pushed that hard. We didn't waste time waiting to see his next reaction or talking about what we should do. We started screaming and running for home as fast as we could. We didn't look around to see if we were being followed. When we finally chanced a look back, there was no one behind us.

We reacted from sheer terror, but I remember thinking that our noise might bring help. However, the main reason for screaming was that these brave warriors were frightened of whistles and screams. Native policemen in their country carried whistles, and they were harsh with any small mistakes made by their own people.

It was such a peaceful evening that our screams carried all the way back to the boys at the orphanage we just left. They walked about two miles to our home because they were worried about something happening to us. We whispered our story, trying not to wake up any more people.

"Did he cut your clothes or your back?" they asked with concern.

Of course, our mother was awake, and she interrupted to let us know right away what she thought. She gave us the devil. Mother would not be shushed. "How dare you? Why weren't you wearing your whistle? Why did you take the shortcut? Why didn't you stay on the main road? It's a half mile longer, but it's safer. Don't you ever do that again. You know you're not supposed to be out after dark." We did know that, but she made sure we really knew it.

We broke three important rules. We weren't wearing our whistles, we didn't stay on the main roads, and we were out after curfew, for which the penalty was suspension from classes for a month. That was a serious punishment because we were already behind with our schooling. We cared very much about our education; we appreciated everything we were taught.

At school the next day there was a lot of whispering about what happened to us, but all the kids kept our secret. We were not suspended from school that day. After a week or so, we breathed a big sigh of relief. "The teachers didn't find out. We're safe."

From our experience, we learned this important lesson: There is a reason for rules.

And no, the clothing on my back wasn't cut and I wasn't hurt. The Masai warrior must have used the blunt edge of his knife because if he wanted to kill us, he certainly could have. He was probably just toying with us.

I was later told, "You needn't have feared the peaceful Masai warriors. They wouldn't kill you because you're not a lion."

28

NURSES TRAINING

GERMANY SURRENDERS
WAR WITH JAPAN GOES ON

Throughout the war, the Mechanical College had been broadcasting Radio Free Europe news on outside speakers that we could hear from our house. From these programs we learned in 1945 that Germany surrendered to the Allies, and the war in

Europe was over. Our people were hugging each other and running to their neighbors shouting, "Our sons are safe. Our fathers have survived. Thank God our brothers are safe."

"The war in Europe is over. Germany is defeated."

It was wonderful news, because now our father, Walter, would be out of harm's way. Everyone in the camp had a relative who was a soldier, and although many lost a husband, son or daughter in the war, everyone was celebrating the end of fighting in Europe.

We were disappointed, though, because Russia was part of the Allies and was not defeated along with Germany. I hated Russia like a poison.

Then another bitter poison went through our camp. I'm not sure how or when we learned this information: the Allies, led by Churchill and Roosevelt, signed the Yalta Agreement with Russia that Poland should remain under Soviet control.

The Polish refugees all expressed the same opinion.

"This agreement is wrong."

"Our Polish men have fought for many years in this accursed war, and those who have survived are now losing their chance to go home to their free country," they argued.

Others sympathized with people in Poland by saying, "I can only imagine how the people who stayed at home must feel."

"Living in Poland will be like being in Russia," my mother stated. "We can't go back home."

All of us were very shocked, hurt and disappointed. With long faces, we went to church and prayed for a miracle to change the outcome for the Polish nation. Some of the priests were so resentful against the English government that they were asked to leave Camp Tengeru, which had been set up by the British.

Having said all of this, I will tell you that I understand the reason behind this appeasement. If Russia had changed sides back to Germany at any time during the fighting, World War II wouldn't have ended any time soon. These world leaders were trying to stop the awful bloodshed of war, thereby saving millions of military and civilian lives. The Allies didn't start this war, and with the exception of Russia, they wanted no territory for themselves. Countries like England sacrificed much at home and suffered many casualties on the battlefield.

Over the next few weeks, we worked at letting go of our deep disappointment. Some people at our camp spoke out against the British for allowing this appeasement to happen.

When peace came to Europe, the Polish women in the English air force were no longer censored and they were finally able to tell us the truth about conditions in Great Britain throughout the war years. A month or so after the armistice, we received a letter from Lottie that opened our eyes and our hearts.

After reading Lottie's letter, we realized how much the English people suffered—much more than we did. She forced us to understand. Because we were helpless to change the Polish situation, my mother told us, "Staying bitter will not improve our lives. We have to move on to the future."

Dear Mother, Millie and Lucille,

    I love you and miss all of you. Sisters, I'm glad you are doing so well with your education in Africa I've been happy and busy in the Air Force. I have felt very much appreciated by the English people. You can't imagine how much they sacrificed for the sake of their country's war effort.
    Whole sections of London were bombed out. Day and night, the air raid sirens went off and everyone scrambled to get to the subway tunnels. Some people slept in these underground stations every night, while others took their chances and stayed in their homes where they might be killed. They shipped their children to safe countries like Canada, Australia and New Zealand.
    The government imposed rationing on everything the civilians ate, and most of the food went to the military personnel. Now that I have been discharged, I'm no longer getting three meals a day prepared for me. I am eating like the average English citizen, and believe me, the air force was given much better food.
    Please write to me soon.

    Your daughter and sister, Lottie

"Now perhaps we can soon be reunited with our dad and sister, and we can all go to America," we said. We didn't know if this dream could come true.

Because I lost three years by not attending school, I had to catch up, and in 1946 I graduated from high school after just two years of study. I got good grades too, I'm proud to say. It was very difficult, but somehow I did it. I wasn't smart. I was stupid, which meant I needed to study day and night. There was very little play time. Lucille also graduated when I did.

Along about this time, our visas to go to the United States expired at the end of two years. I'm not sure about the date. If I had been smart, I would have made notes or kept a journal, but we were so busy just existing from day to day that we didn't even think about a diary.

Although we knew the politicians in America were trying to renew our visas, we also knew there was a quota on the number of citizens from any one country allowed into the United States. We had to go on with our lives in Africa.

After graduation, Lucille went on to teacher's college, and I took an eight-month course in nurse's training. Eight doctors gave us lessons. We also worked without pay in the hospital to get the experience. I'll never forget the first time I saw a childbirth. One student nurse fainted, and they carried her out while I stayed to help.

After our course, there was a final exam on Friday, the thirteenth, in early summer of 1947. I don't remember the month. No one wanted to take an important test on that unlucky day, but another girl and I decided to get it over with. "Luck is with us," we said when we learned both of us passed

Photo #4

Millie in nurse's uniform - 1947

with very good grades. Four of us graduating with high honors were hired at the large local hospital, where we worked one of the three shifts: morning, afternoon, or midnight. We were required to rotate our work hours.

Our uniforms were white linen and they needed to be washed, starched and ironed, using an iron made hot over our improvised stove. Stockings, comfortable shoes, and stiff caps also had to be white.

The doctors, nurses and patients were all friendly, with a pleasant "good morning" or "good afternoon" at the beginning of each shift. They cared more for others than they did for themselves. I felt privileged to become part of this group. I was young and healthy, and I could now help sick patients, especially older people.

The first time I got paid, I was so proud because this was the first money I earned. Now I was truly an adult. Our salaries were very low because the African economy was so poor, and I was required to buy my own uniforms, shoes and caps.

After I went to work, I continued to live with my mother and sister in the beehive house, and we spent what little was left of my salary on living expenses. Now we could buy extra fruit at the market, and we got special things like fabric for clothes, which the dressmaker sewed. I wasn't able to save much from my nurse's pay.

Alhough I wasn't getting rich, I loved my profession. One doctor called me his *pupilka,* which translates into his "ward," but he said it meant I was his favorite nurse. When he went on his rounds in the morning, he always said, "Millie, come with me." He was a very good-looking man.

I wasn't afraid to do any of the jobs I was given. I gave shots or other medicine, and it also didn't bother me to prepare the bodies when someone died. One night on the midnight shift, a man passed away. Another nurse and I were washing him when his penis became very stiff with rigor mortis, and it was as erect as the mast on a sailboat. We were new nurses, and this had never come up in our training. The other nurse looked at me for guidance and I looked at her.

"I don't think we can take him to the morgue with the sheet poking straight up in the middle of his body," I said.

We were giggling even while we were concerned about what to do. She asked, "Can we push it down?"

Gently folding the penis over, we tried to get it to stay down, but the answer to her question was, "No, we can't."

We tried waiting for a few minutes. There was no downward movement. Again we tried gently bending the penis, but it popped right back up again.

We knew we needed to get him down to the cooler part of the hospital soon.

"Let's take him to the morgue the way he is and hope that by morning all will be smooth," we finally decided.

In the morning the doctor came and pronounced the man dead. He didn't say anything was wrong, and we didn't ask.

There were other experiences. One night I was taking care of an old lady of about 80 who was dying. I was 20 years of age, and to me she was very old. She knew she was dying, and she liked me. She owned a cross on a chain which she brought all the way from Poland. She told me, "Take the cross off my neck because I want to give it to you."

I took her necklace because that was her wish, but later I had second thoughts and gave it back to her family when they came to accept the body. I knew that cross would mean a lot to them.

There were also a lot of young people dying in Africa. One of our teachers didn't cover her head when she went outside in the blazing sun and she got a bad case of sunstroke. When she lost her mind, she was locked in a room with bars because she was a danger to others. We felt sorry for her, and someone said, "Perhaps she would be better off if she died."

I was working as a nurse when we received word that Indiana Congressman Meden renewed our visas. Transportation in the world was returning to normal, but we waited in line along with all the other people wanting to travel.

Because in Africa I worked at a job I loved with people who liked me as much as I liked them, I wasn't sure about going to America. I loved the older nurses and the doctors.

If we moved to America, I would miss the security we knew in Africa. We lived in a home provided for us. There were no worries because everything was organized in our camp, like the housing, classes, food, entertainment and activities. The bad parts about Africa—the mosquitoes—the heat—washing our clothes in the cold stream—we would be happy to give up.

As far as we could tell, everyone was happy in each of the 22 Polish camps in Africa, all of which seemed to be as well run as Camp Kondoa and Camp Tengeru.

In Siberia I had been forced to work as a slave; in Africa my carefree years came back. This was definitely the best part of my youth.

29

LUCILLE IN TEACHER'S COLLEGE

OTHER VOICES: Lucille

I was very glad to go back to school in Africa; I finished the third and fourth year of high school in one year. The work was very accelerated. Even when we took a month's vacation during the hottest seasons, we were required to read five or six books and write a report about them, which we turned in to our teacher when school resumed.

We studied so hard that I remember telling my mother, "Because I have so much homework, I only get an hour's sleep a night."

"Now, Lucille, are you sure about that?"

"Well, that's the way it seems to me."

I was three years behind for my age when we got to Africa. All the students were very motivated to study hard, because we missed a whole year when Poland was invaded and we were abducted. Then we lost another year in Siberia, and a third year when we were freed and traveling around Russia and Iran.

After graduating from high school, I went to teacher's college for two years. Then in the last half of my second year of college, I was a substitute teacher for one hour a day. I went to the school and checked the blackboard for my assignment. Every day I was given a different subject and a new grade to instruct. After finding that classroom and textbook, I had a total of one hour to read the lesson and teach it. If I didn't understand the content of the lesson quickly enough, I was required to improvise with some information about that subject.

I might be working in a class of first or sixth grade children, or even high school students. If it was a history class, I taught the kids something about history for about 15 minutes. Then I asked them to write a report about the lesson, which they gave to their regular instructor. In that way, she knew what I had taught her students.

Of course, I was required to do make-up work from the college class I missed while I was substituting.

At the end of 1947, I got my teacher's certificate. This meant I could be a teacher if I went back to Poland. At this time we were still not sure when we would be able to go to America, and we still clung to the hope that Poland could again be rid of Communism.

A free homeland was only our dream, as my father proved when he was in England after the war. Some of his friends went to Poland after their military service, and they ended up back in Siberia. We definitely made the right decision not to return to our beloved Poland.

30

LOTTIE AND WALTER
IN ENGLAND

OTHER VOICES: Lottie

Most of us didn't date while we were in England. Instead we went out as a group of men and women. I was afraid to get romantically entangled with any man while I was in the air force because by this time I knew my family was trying to get to the United States, and I wanted to be reunited with them. In one of her letters, my sister Millie gave another reason for not dating servicemen. She said, "I'm careful not to get too involved with any of the men with whom I'm corresponding in case they don't survive the war."

Finally in 1945 the war in Europe was ended and I knew my father was safe. After the armistice, four of us Polish servicewomen shared one bedroom at a majestic villa that was surrounded by beautiful gardens. England still was home to a lot of extra people, and the large estates provided lodging for many of us. These houses were called hostels.

I was working at the camp near Lincolnshire when the war with Japan ended, and I and my fellow Polish servicewomen were honorably discharged. I found myself with nowhere to go. I knew I didn't want to be in Poland under

Communism, and it was very difficult to get to the United States. At this time my mother and sisters were still in Africa, and my father had not yet moved to England. The only thing I could do was to stay in England at a resettlement camp, where we were given job training for civilian life.

In 1947, my dad and I were reunited in England, and I went to see him. He was smoking and he offered me a cigarette.

"No, thank you." I shook my head.

He said, "I thought all the air force women learned to smoke." He was testing me.

"Well, I don't."

"Good. I don't want you to be smoking," he told me.

"But Father, you smoke."

"Yes, but I wish I didn't. Smoking got me through some tough times during the war," he explained. He didn't say what that meant, but I could guess.

I told him, "We got cigarettes very easily during the war, but I always took my cigarettes and exchanged them for chocolate."

He nodded his head and laughed.

Father and I discussed the rationing that was still on all food items. "Even when I can afford to buy, I can't get food without a ration coupon," Father said. "I'm lucky to be working as a cook in our Polish club, because I can eat there."

"Yes, I've come to appreciate how well-fed we were in the air force during the war, with our three good meals a day," I added.

The economy in England wasn't good for many years after the war ended, and there were few good jobs. Of course, the British managers hired their own people first, so I wasn't able to start working until 1948. Several of us were still living on the estate and we were taken by bus to Dunstable where we found jobs at a printing company. I ran a special machine similar to a lithograph. Each sheet of paper was individually printed in those days.

My job as a lithographer didn't pay very well, and I couldn't afford to buy fruit unless it was already starting to rot. After paying the rent and buying my food, I had nothing left to spend. My father sympathized with my predicament.

He decided, "You need to find a better job. I'll write to my friends in London."

Dear friends,

My daughter and her girlfriend, recently discharged from the Royal Air Force, will be going to London to look for work. They don't have the money for a hotel. Would it be possible for them to stay with you for a couple of weeks while they job hunt? Thanking you in advance,

Walter Zygmunt

Father's friends wrote to me.

Dear Lottie,

    Because we think so much of your father, we would be pleased to provide temporary housing for you and your friend. Let us know when you will arrive and we'll have a room ready for the two of you.
    We remain, Walter's friends, James and Rose Wilson

    When my girlfriend and I went to London to look for work, we both found a job sewing men's suits. I had taken a sewing class in Poland, so I was qualified. There was a big demand for clothing in England after the war because for six or seven years the manufacturers had converted to making military uniforms. Everyone's wardrobe was worn out, and they had nothing left to wear. Also, to get revenue for the British economy, we were told that most of these new clothes were exported to Canada and Australia.
    We found a one-room apartment near our jobs, which was lucky because we could walk to work.

On our warm days off, we enjoyed strolling in Woodbine Park across the street.

However, our living space was hot during the summer and cold during the winter months. To warm our room, there was a gas heater that would flash on briefly when we inserted a shilling into a coin slot. This greedy furnace swallowed our money and gave back scant warmth in return. It also served as our hot water heater and cooking stove. Most of the time we ate sandwiches of bread with tomatoes or other vegetables because this simple meal did not require cooking.

The bathroom for all the occupants of this four-apartment building was in the basement, and its heater also worked when it was fed with shillings. It was so hungry for our money that my roommate and I learned to conserve its energy by filling the tub with hot water, jumping in for a quick bath, then washing our clothes and sheets in the same warm water.

"Let's see how fast we can do our bathing and washing," one of us would challenge the other.

Our new jobs in London paid much better than our lithography work in Dunstable. Although our expenses were also higher, my friend agreed with me when I decided, "I'm so happy we made this move to London."

"Thanks for your help, Father."

31

FLIGHT TO AMERICA

January, 1948
   My dear wife, Stephanie, and daughters, Millie and Lucille,

   I was happy to get your letter telling me about your plane tickets to America. Stephanie, when you see your sister, Appolonia, please tell her thank you from me. Without her sponsoring you and buying your tickets, you wouldn't be able to go to America so soon.
   I do have one worry, and that is about your two-day layover in Egypt. Millie and Lucille, don't waste this wonderful opportunity for you and your mother. Don't take any chances in Cairo by trusting strangers. Don't go along with anyone you meet. Please listen to what I'm telling you. Be very careful in the sun and eat only at the hotel or on the plane. If you get sick and miss your flight, you may not get another chance.
   All of us want to be reunited some day in America. It has been such a long time since I have seen all of you. Every day I picture in my mind how good it will be when we meet again soon.

      Your husband and father, Walter

Father wrote that letter to us right before we left for America. I listened to him, but I was not ready to think about what might happen in Egypt. All my concerns were about our friends in the jungle of Africa. Because we had been together for five years, the people in Africa became my family, all 2000 of them. I knew I would miss their company. Also, I loved my job, and I enjoyed having my own money for the first time in my life.

I was afraid to leave the security of our Camp Tengeru because we didn't know what we might find in America. We had never met our relatives. We asked ourselves, "What if they are mean?" "Where are we going?" "Will the Polish Americans accept us?" "Will we have trouble learning the English language?" "Will we be able to get good jobs?" Well, we decided to take a chance. All of our lives we had been taking chances.

We didn't know this at the time we were planning our future, but the camps in Africa would be disbanded and the remaining Polish refuges would be brought to England the following May and June. If we had been able to foresee the future, our decision to go to the United States would have been easier to make.

In January, 1948, we became the first family from Camp Tengeru to leave Africa. Our truck driver drove us to Nairobi, in Kenya, and from there we flew first class on Trans World Airlines to Cairo, Egypt, where there was a two-day layover.

When we checked into a hotel in Cairo, Mother gave us Father's letter saying, "Read this again and think about it."

"*Don't take any chances in Cairo by trusting strangers. Do not go along with anyone you don't know,*" he had written. "Do we have a reputation for taking adventurous chances?" I asked Lucille. "Both Mother and Father seem to think so," she answered. "Maybe we should listen to them."

Later that day, while on a stroll outside our hotel in Cairo, Lucille and I met a handsome man who asked, "Would you like to go with me for a tour of the city? We can also take a camel ride out to the pyramids."

Of course we wanted to do those things. Who wouldn't?

But we were listening to Father's letter and Mother's words. "Thank you for your offer, but no thank you," we answered.

After two uneventful days in Cairo, we re-boarded the plane and flew to Italy, then to Spain, then to the Azore Islands, and finally on to New York City. The same plane made that many stops. It was a long flight and it was cold on the plane, but we made ourselves as comfortable as possible and napped when we could.

When we first touched the ground in New York in 1948, we knew we were very lucky, even though we were not yet United States citizens. The Americans we saw wore their freedom like their clothes. There was a spirit of independence and energy about the way they walked with assurance and made eye contact with anyone. It was as if they were saying, "I can do anything I want. I don't have to listen to anyone else. No one tells me what to do.

As long as I'm not hurting anyone else, I have to answer only to myself."

In New York we went through the United States customs where they checked our papers and our luggage to make sure we weren't smuggling anything in. "We certainly can't hide much, because we have very few possessions—mostly just dirty clothes," I told my mother.

We went from the hottest climate in equatorial Africa to one of the coldest winters in the history of New York. My mother bought wool material in Africa, which she took to a dressmaker who sewed short coats for all of us to wear.

In the heat of Africa, it was hard to imagine wool clothing, but we agreed with Mother when she decided, "We'll need warm coats when we get to America."

After Mother, Lucille and I were processed through customs, an agent from our travel bureau met us at the airport and took us, suitcases and all, to a restaurant for breakfast. At that time, we spoke very little English, and we had a hard time communicating with him, but we got by.

Our departure time on the train to Chicago was not until late that afternoon, so the agent gave us a riding tour of New York City. I was too excited to remember very much about that whole day.

At the railroad station, the travel agent gave us money for food and put us on a passenger train with reclining seats so we could sleep overnight. Except for the time I was lost for a day in Russia and I rode in the Communists' premium class railroad car, it was the first time I experienced a passenger train with bathrooms.

In the early morning we woke up and saw Chicago for the first time. We didn't like what we saw because the days-old snow looked black and dirty. We had never seen anything like that before. From the time we were abducted in Poland until we arrived in Chicago, we had been moved to a new place on:

1 Four rides inside boxcars
2 One ride outside a boxcar
3 Four trucks fitted with benches
4 Two buses
5 Two sleds pulled by horses
6 Three wagons pulled by oxen or horses
7 Two barges
8 Two passenger cars
9 One ship
10 One large airliner
11 One passenger train for real people
12 Ambulances
13 Plus many, many walking miles

For eight years, we had traveled through Poland, Russia, Siberia in Russia, Kazakhstan and Turkmenistan in the Soviet Union, Iran, Pakistan (then part of India), India, Tanganyika (now called Tanzania), Kenya, Egypt, Italy, Spain, the Azores and the United States. We had lived in Europe, Asia, Africa and North America—four different continents.

Often the members of our family had suffered illnesses like malaria, dysentery, typhoid fever, sunstroke, malnutrition and seasickness.

And we had endured.

32

EXPLOSION OF WELCOME

It was calm and quiet on the train from New York that Friday afternoon and night in January of 1948. As we stepped off the arrival platform in Chicago and started down the exit stairs that Saturday morning, we walked into an explosion—of cheers—of curiosity—of commotion—of hugs—of questions—of laughter—of acceptance—of noise— of tears—of celebration—of generosity. It was an explosion of welcome.

There were about 25 people, all of whom were talking at once, but from looking at pictures, we instantly knew which one of them must be Aunt Appolonia. She was the director, producer and fundraiser for this production. For four years she planned and organized the first Red Cross phone calls, our visas, the correspondence, the travel arrangements, and now the welcoming committee. She was there with her husband Kasper and all of their children.

Uncle Ignatc and Uncle Stanley came with their wives and growing families. Because Lucille and I had never met any of these people, we couldn't place the faces with the names we memorized. They didn't know us either. They asked, "Are you Millie? Are you Lucille?"

Most of the conversation was in Polish, and we soon felt comfortable with our new-found relatives.

After some discussion it was decided, "Stephanie, Millie and Lucille will each ride in a different car as our whole group drives in a caravan to Aunt Appolonia's house in Hammond, Indiana."

An hour later the party exploded again with even more relatives, friends, and neighbors. The house erupted with an overflowing of people, food and generosity. Everyone was curious to meet us and fascinated by our story.

Aunt Appolonia spread the word that we would be coming to America with nothing. Everyone brought clothes from their attics to give us. Dresses and coats, blouses and skirts, shoes and boots, socks and underwear, in many different sizes, were spread out two or three layers deep over the beds and dressers in the bedrooms.

Mother, Lucille and I went shopping in this well-stocked ladies clothing store, finding things to fit each of us. My cousin gave me her new dress, but when I modeled the dress for the relatives, they began teasing, "You'll have to grow six inches, Millie, to wear your tall cousin's skirt."

"It can be shortened," was the final decision, and I owned a brand new garment. The dress was black with large red roses, which wasn't my kind of style, but I wore it for a long time. It was beautiful because it was a gift from my cousin and because it was new.

The kitchen was equally well stocked with salads, breads, casseroles, cheeses and meats. There were pies, cakes and cookies for dessert. Everyone must have realized that Aunt Appolonia would have more people to feed at her party and in the next few weeks.

The following morning, Sunday, we went to Appolonia's church, St. Casimir's. Because we were the first of many Polish immigrants who later came to Hammond, Indiana, we got a lot of attention. Some people were gaping out of car windows to see what we looked like. As we walked down the aisle to our seats inside the church, I noticed an increased buzzing of whispered talk.

I overheard, "I thought they would be much thinner because we heard they were starving."

"Their skin is so dark brown. Their hair is so light blonde."

Some people, not wanting to be rude, were staring at us out of the corners of their eyes. After the service, many went out of their way to say, "Welcome to America," or "We're glad you're here," or "Good morning."

That day we learned one thing: Our worries about being accepted by the Polish American people were groundless, because it was like we had lived here all of our lives.

Sunday was a day for seeing people and relaxing after our long trip. Monday morning we started looking for work. I talked to St. Margaret's Hospital to see about being a nurse in this country. They said, "You have to go for more schooling, and while you are training, you will be required to do 1000 hours of hospital volunteer work, after which you will have to take a test." At that time I couldn't read English, and there was no chance that I could pass an exam. I wouldn't be able to work in my nursing profession here in this country. I would have to find other employment.

Aunt Appolonia told us, "You don't have to pay me back for what I spent on your transportation here."

Mother, Lucille and I talked about what to do. "Uncle Kasper is not in the best of health. Your aunt and uncle aren't wealthy people. They don't have a high income, and they have a small home. It wouldn't be right to accept their kind offer," my mother decided.

Her daughters agreed, "We will pay her back."

Now there was an urgency to our job seeking. Lucille and I applied at a shirt factory not far from Aunt Appolonia's house, and three days after we came to America, my sister and I went to work sewing collars on men's shirts. I needed to be careful to keep the point of the collar and to not break the thread. We made 60 cents per hour, but we could work overtime for piece work. I always worked until they chased me from the factory before they closed for the night. I made big money for 1948, about $10 a day clear. When we received our first paychecks, we felt very rich.

Our thrill about our first earned money in America was forgotten when Mother got very sick with a high fever and chills. Aunt Appolonia called her doctor, and he made a house call. He wasn't sure what was wrong with her until we told him, "We think she has malaria."

"People don't get malaria in the United States in January," he said.

When we told him, "We just arrived from Africa a week ago," we had his attention. He put Stephanie in St. Margaret's Hospital, where a blood test confirmed that she did indeed have malaria. She needed blood transfusions, and again my cousins from Chicago came to the rescue to donate five pints of blood. Lucille and I couldn't give blood because we had suffered from malaria in Africa. We would never be able to be a donor again.

My mother was hospitalized for three weeks, and Lucille and I now would have even more bills to pay, so this was quite a setback for us.

With the three of us in addition to her own family, Aunt Appolonia's two-bedroom house was very crowded. I slept in the warm basement on a comfortable couch, while Mother and Lucille shared a sleeper sofa upstairs in the living room.

Everyone agreed with our decision. "The time has come for us to get our own place."

Again Aunt solved the problem by finding a small rental apartment nearby. There was a tiny living room, a kitchen, two bedrooms and a bathroom. It was a bargain at $50 a month, probably because it was so dirty, but we took brushes and soap to wash the walls and floors, and soon it was squeaky clean.

In the middle of the kitchen floor was a big heating stove. One of my Chicago cousins came to see us, took one look at the heater, and decided, "That stove is too old and too dangerous." He went to the hardware store where he bought a brand new cast iron model. It was beautiful. He installed the stove and brought us some wood and coal, and we heated the apartment. He also taught us how to safely use his new gift.

My aunt gave us a single bed for my mother. Lucille and I slept on the floor for a while until we bought a bedroom set, which was the first purchase we made in America. Again relatives and neighbors came to help, giving us everything we needed to start housekeeping. Old tables and chairs, ironing boards, silverware and dishes, pots and pans—these were all gifts from generous people. The knives and forks didn't match and some of the dishes were chipped, but we certainly didn't care. Without them, we owned nothing. We appreciated everything.

There was a grocery store across the street from our apartment, where it was handy for us to buy food, because we obviously couldn't drive. Someone gave us $3, others gave us $5, $2, $1, or whatever they could spare. Everyone gave us some money to get started. In Africa Mother had exchanged our English money into $27 in United States currency. This was what we saved from our salaries and from what our father sent to us.

We were comfortably settled into our new home in America, but we needed to make money to settle our $3600 debt to Aunt Appolonia for our transportation from Africa to America, and we wanted to support our mother and ourselves.

Learning English became another job for us. When we first came to this country, we took an English course at night school in Hammond High because we needed to work during the day. Later we went to another night school that was started on State Street because there were more people needing English lessons.

After several months, Lucille got a better job making refrigerator parts on an assembly line at General American in East Chicago. Our neighbor was a supervisor there, so he gave her a job and a ride to work. She was now making the princely sum of $1.10 per hour. My aunt found a better job for me at Junior Toys making children's bicycles. The pay was higher, and sometimes I got overtime. I worked six days a week. It was too far to walk, but my aunt gave me a falling-apart bicycle to ride to work. In Poland we had owned one bicycle for our whole family, and I knew how to ride a two-wheeler. At this job I met friendly Polish girls who invited me to go out with their group of men and women to movies or dances, and now I had a social life.

Each time we heard about a better-paying job, we applied. After a couple of years, I went to work at General American with my sister. Each morning we caught a bus, which ran just once per hour, on the other side of some railroad tracks from our home. Sometimes a mile-long train was blocking the tracks, and we didn't want to miss our bus and be late for work.

"How long will it take us to run around the train?"

"About fifteen minutes."

"When is the bus due to come?"

"In five minutes."

"Shall we crawl over the cars or under them?" was the only decision.

There was nothing for us to do except crawl underneath the train where the cars were connected. We reasoned that the engineer would release the brakes with a loud puff of air pressure, giving us warning before the wheels started rolling. Or so we hoped.

It was taking a stupid chance, but, "We have no choice," we agreed.

These trains blocked the tracks every couple of weeks, and we got pretty good at crawling under them.

We were desperate to earn money, and Mother helped as soon as she regained her health. She found a job as a short-order cook in a rooming house and bar/restaurant. She worked from 7:00 in the morning until 10:00 at night, with a break in the middle when she rested. The owner let newly-arrived immigrants live and eat on credit until they found jobs and paid him back. He was kind to Mother, and she stayed for seven or eight years. He paid both his and her share of her Social Security.

Aunt Appolonia didn't charge interest on the $3600 we owed her, and every week we carefully recorded each payment we made to her. In less than two years we paid off Mother's hospital bill and our debt to our aunt, all the while supporting ourselves. I was very proud of that. Lucille and I put all of our money together. After that we budgeted for the rent and for our living expenses, and we used the rest of our money to pay off our aunt. For the first few months we went without a phone or a refrigerator.

The relatives asked, "Where did they get all that money to get out of debt so fast? How can they be making that much?"

We paid off our debt quickly because we didn't spend money on anything unnecessary.

My Aunt Appolonia gave a better answer. "All I know is they're not stealing, because if they were, they'd be in jail."

33

SOCIAL LIFE

Lucille and I didn't work all the time. We enjoyed a busy social life too.

When we arrived in the United States after the war, we were immediately accepted by the Polish American people as one of their own, as equals. There was absolutely no snobbery there. They gave us a chance. I love those people, and I would do anything for them.

My sister and I joined a group of young Polish Americans who organized dances, picnics, bus trips to beaches, and other fun activities.

The boys knew we didn't have a car, so they stopped for us and gave us rides to parties. When the driver picked us up at our home, there might be as many as eight guys and gals in the car. When we first arrived in America, we were a curiosity because we were not born here, and all the men wanted to be dance partners with the new and exciting immigrants. Sometimes two or three guys asked me for a dance at the same time. We got a lot of attention. Also, there were more men than women at these parties, so we immediately enjoyed ourselves.

Some weekends we danced all evening at Danceland in Whiting, then went to a nightclub in Calumet City, then went home for a few hours of sleep, then attended Mass at 7:00 Sunday morning. In the afternoon we might have a picnic on our

Photo #5

Millie as chairman - 1950

schedule. "There can't be too many activities for me," I told my mother.

At that time Hammond was celebrating its centennial. Our club hired a professional dance instructor, and our whole group performed on stage, but my partner, George, and I did a solo *krakowiak* dance for this celebration.

I had danced a little bit in Africa, but not enough to be good. When I first came to the United States, many Polish American friends, men and women, showed me different steps and moves. I also met Casey, a bachelor about ten years older than my 21 years. He was a very good dancer who often asked me to be his partner, teaching me a lot about the jitterbug, polka and waltz.

I was enjoying life as a single woman. I decided, "Let other women have husbands and responsibility." Every weekend I went out with a different guy. Honest to God, I was having such a good time. These were now the fun-loving teen years I missed by being in Siberia and Africa. I was in no hurry to get married.

And then I met Stephan Rytel.

34

OUR COURTSHIP

The *Paczkowy Bal* is a traditional Polish custom that some local churches used as a fund raiser right before Lent. In 1949, St. John's Cantius Church sold tickets for their ball in the harbor part of East Chicago. Coffee and alcoholic drinks were for sale, as well as bismarks, which are rolls filled with jelly.

Lucille and I were going to this ball with a newcomer friend of ours, who came to our house with his cousin who owned a car, and the four of us drove to the dance.

My sister was dancing, but I didn't want to be the other man's partner, so I was sitting all alone on one of the benches that lined the walls. Some man came over and introduced himself. "Hi. My name is Stephan Rytel. May I have this dance?"

He walked with a limp, and I wasn't too impressed at first. Who wants to be with a man who limps? I was particular, like we all are, but I wanted to dance. I said, "Yes, you may have this dance—and I'm Millie."

"Have you just come to America?" he opened the conversation. He could tell I was a recent immigrant, and I also knew he was not an American man. We started waltzing, and I liked the graceful way he moved. At that time I didn't know too much about dancing. Each guy interprets the music differently, and I was insecure about following him.

Finally he said to me, "You're OK."

We talked in Polish about where we came from in the old country. We had both been deported to Russia. I was taken in February of 1940. Stephan told me, "I was abducted, along with my mother and sister, four months later in June, right after I finished just one year of high school."

We told each other how we got out of Russia and where we were during the war. We discussed where our families were now. However, we didn't bring up our worst times in Siberia. It was a degrading experience that hurt too much, and all of us who lived through the awful events just wanted to forever bury all the memories. Stephan wouldn't even tell me where in the Soviet Union he was taken and what work he did there. Somehow, forgetting the details helped to lessen the pain. It was better to remember the good things that happened since then.

Mostly we learned about where and how each of us traveled to get to the United States. Stephan told me, "I arrived from England on a passenger ship, and I took a train from New York to Hammond."

He was not at all bitter or resentful about his capture. He was a person who adjusted to whatever circumstances life threw at him.

We both wanted to share so much about ourselves, and we talked all night. At the end of the evening, he asked to take me home. I said, "Maybe, maybe not."

I asked my sister if I should let Stephan take me home. She said, "Don't you dare go with him; you don't know him. He could kidnap you."

When I went back to Stephan to tell him I couldn't go with him because I was afraid, he understood. "There is no pressure. May I have your telephone number instead?" he asked.

Because I liked this man so much, I decided, "That's a good idea. Let's exchange phone numbers."

The next day he called to tell me about a St. Valentine's Day dance at Danceland the next Wednesday. All day I had been reflecting about what a good time I'd enjoyed with this Stephan Rytel, and I wanted to date him. In spite of my family's warnings that I didn't know him, I said, "Yes, I'd love to go with you."

When I was reminded by Lucille that he walked with a limp, I said, "Oh, that limp isn't too bad."

At this time I worked at the Kraft Company in Chicago. I got up at 4:00 in the morning to catch the train into Chicago, and then I walked twelve blocks to work. Darkness or sunshine, blizzard or rain, that was my routine. I was supposed to be home by 6:30 p.m., but when Stephan called my house, my mother told him, "She isn't home yet."

When I finally arrived, I hoped he would call again. He didn't. In those days girls didn't call boys. I waited for about two minutes—then two more—then one more. I didn't care if women weren't supposed to call men. I liked him so much that I telephoned this man. I asked Stephan, "Is there a chance we can still go out?"

He agreed, "Of course we can."

I changed my clothes and fixed myself up, and when he stopped for me a half hour later, he brought me a corsage for St. Valentine's Day.

I loved Stephan from the first time I met him. He was everything I was looking for, because he was very gentle and thoughtful, always thinking about me or other people. When Mother asked why I liked him so much, I replied, "Because he is just the right height, and I don't have to wear high heels when I dance with him." The truth was that he was the best man I ever knew.

Stephan kissed me that night, and that was it. "What limp?"

35

STEPHAN RYTEL

In northeast Poland in a country village called Ciemiatycze, near Bialystok, Stephen Rytel was born on January 3, 1924. When he came to the United States in 1949, the date on his Polish papers was entered the European way as 3-1-24, and the American customs officers wrote March 1, 1924 as the official birth date on his immigration documents.

His parents were more affluent than their neighbors, and they owned a big farm for which they hired many workers. When World War II broke out, Stephan had finished his first year of high school. His father was serving in the Polish army when he was arrested by the Russians, and for a long time his family didn't know where their father and husband was.

Stephan was abducted to Siberia with his mother and sister in June of 1940, four months after we were taken.

Like other Polish men and boys, the only way Stephan could get out of Russia in 1941 was to join the army. Stephan was in the junior army for a year or two before qualifying for the regular army. He lied about his age, adding two years, so he would be old enough to get into the *Pulk Ulanow,* a unit of

young men with good looks and physiques. They
marched in parades, saluting to the officers. He
didn't have a high rank because he was too young.
His highest-ranking commanding officer, a man
named Sikorski, was very intelligent. He was the
Polish representative to the Allies, dealing with
Roosevelt, with Stalin, and with the English.
General Sikorski also became the Prime Minister of
the Polish government-in-exile.

After their release from prison camp, Stephan
left his mother and sister in Russia when he was
drafted into the Polish unit of the British army. He
was very worried about them, but somehow,
through his connections in the army, he learned they
were able to get back to Poland. There they were
reunited with their husband and father, and the three
family members went back to their old farm.

A couple of months later, his sister, weakened
by malnutrition in Russia, became very sick with
pneumonia and died at the age of 21. There was no
help for sick people in Poland during the war.
Stephan was then his parents' only child.

When Stephan was 18 years old, his unit was
sent to Italy. The Polish Army, commanded by
General Anders, was fighting the battle of Monte
Cassino, together with the Indians, New Zealanders,
Canadians, French, Americans and English.

I listened as Stephan spoke, "All the armies
were ordered to stop fighting, but our Polish Army,
comprised almost entirely of former slave laborers,
volunteered for the suicide mission to capture the
top of the mountain. We were so determined to rid
the world of the twin evils of Russia and Germany,
which all of us witnessed first hand, that we didn't

care if we lived or died. To us, the battle at Monte Cassino became the symbol for everything morally wrong in this world. We couldn't be stopped by anyone or anything."

Many men were killed, but the surviving soldiers defeated the German army and mounted their Polish national flag on the castle at the top, and, as of this writing, it is still there. This victory was important because it opened for the Allies the only north-south road to Rome.

Stephan was gunned down by German machine guns the night before the end of the battle. He lost consciousness, but in the morning the dew revived him. He heard some Red Cross workers walking by looking for wounded soldiers, but they couldn't see him because he was covered with rubble and dirt. Somehow he managed to throw a pebble at the rescuers to get their attention.

"Where did that stone come from?" Stephan heard the man's question. "There must be someone here under the rubble. Here he is. Take care now. He looks to be in bad shape."

The rescuers dug Stephan out and took him down the mountain on a stretcher to the hospital. His guts were all out of his body. The nurses cleaned him up as best they could, and a Polish doctor sewed him back together again. An English doctor, a specialist in infections, also took care of him. Stephan asked them, "Am I going to live?"

The doctors replied, "We did everything human hands can do. From here on, it's up to the man upstairs."

He also had shrapnel in his back. Later in his life when he went for X-rays, he explained to his doctors exactly what happened to him. Stephan spent two months in an Italian hospital before he was shipped to England for another six months. For that whole time he was fed intravenously, and he was given no food or water.

After he got well, he was discharged from the hospital and from the Polish Army. He then went to mechanic's school to learn a trade.

Stephan later said to me, "I felt like a prince when I was in England. Because there were so many British men who didn't return from the war, the ladies outnumbered the men at parties. I went out dancing every night with a different woman."

Because Stephan took lessons, he was a good dancer. Another skill he learned in England was how to drive a car.

Stephan came to the United States in 1949 with no possessions at all. The English government helped the Polish soldiers re-settle by paying for their transportation to whatever new country they adopted. His Aunt Marie and Uncle Henry sponsored their nephew, and he lived with them in the harbor part of East Chicago. His uncle helped him get a job at Inland Steel just two days after he arrived, because his aunt's brother was a supervisor there.

He also helped Aunt Marie and Uncle Henry at their store. When Stephan first started at Inland Steel, his uncle lent him the money to buy an old red Ford so he would have transportation to work. He told me, "That car burnt so much oil—I carried extra cans of it in my trunk."

During all this time, Stephan hadn't written to his parents in Poland. He knew from personal experience how the Russians spied on people and sent them to prison for the smallest suspicions. He was afraid they would get into trouble with the Communist government if he sent any message from America. When his mother and father were questioned about their son's whereabouts, they could reply honestly, "We don't know where he is."

36

WALTER IN ENGLAND

We corresponded several times a week with my father, Walter Zygmunt, and after World War II ended, he asked in each letter, "How are we going to get back together again?"

When Stephanie came to the United States, she agreed that Walter and Lottie would have to come to America too, and this became our family's goal.

The British government shipped their entire army home after the war. Also, England did not abandon on the battlefield all the Polish servicemen who fought with the Allies, and 25,000 surviving Polish soldiers went to Britain, where they were accepted with respect. They were given housing and jobs. There were a few Polish ex-soldiers, like my cousin, who married English women, but most men were waiting for their families to be brought to Great Britain. Many of these people were resettled in some permanent location like America, Australia or Canada.

When Walter first arrived in Great Britain, he lived in a barrack in Ireland, but he soon moved to England where he found a job as a chef in a Polish club. He knew Lottie's address because of their correspondence during the war. Lottie and Father met in England and attended Polish parties or meetings together, but they didn't live in the same house.

To get to the United States, my father and Lottie needed to find a politician to get visas for them. The American government wanted to make certain that the newcomers wouldn't become a burden to the country. Therefore all immigrants needed a sponsor. This responsibility was not to be taken lightly, because some people were burned by new immigrants who refused to work and thus became dependents of their benefactors.

My mother, sister and I couldn't take this responsibility for Walter and Lottie because we hadn't been here long enough to become citizens. My generous cousin from Chicago owned a restaurant and could guarantee employment for Walter and Lottie, and he became their sponsor.

Of course, in America Father never lived anywhere except with us, and he found a job on his own. Although his sponsor didn't have to do anything except sign the paper, Walter was grateful to this Chicago cousin because Father and Lottie couldn't have come to America without him.

37

VISA FOR WALTER AND LOTTIE

OTHER VOICES: Lottie

My father applied for a visa to come to America while he was still in Italy, but when he came to England he was required to reapply, which delayed our whole emigration process. At this time I also applied for my visa at the American Embassy on Grosvenor Square. We were told, "When your visas

Photo #6

Walter and Lottie - 1949

arrive, you can go to the United States together."

I worked on Grosvenor Street near the American Embassy, and many times I went there

during my lunch hour and inquired about our visas.
"Are you bothering them?" my father asked.
"Yes, it would be fair to say that I'm bugging
the embassy staff." I admitted.

In 1949, my roommate emigrated to America.
This was wonderful news for her, but not good for
me because I could no longer afford to pay for my
apartment by myself. Father came to my rescue
again by paying part of my rent.

At the time we were trying to emigrate, the
strict quota on immigrants from Poland was set so
low that it took a long time to get to the United
States. All of us could have gotten to the states
much sooner under the Austrian quota, because both
my mother and father were born under their flag
when they occupied Poland. My mother
remembered when she was a child in school, and
the students opened each day by singing the
Austrian national anthem.

By the time my father found out about the
Austrian quota from other Polish people who used
it, we were already in the United States. We thought
we had everything figured out, but we learned there
were some important things we didn't know
because we didn't have access to all the
information.

I had been working at my sewing job for about
two years when we were notified that both my
father and I received our visas to come to America.
For four years I dreamed about and waited to hear
this news.

Our next step was to be X-rayed and examined
by an American doctor to make sure we were
healthy.

In 1951, after we were already in America, the United States government enlarged its quota for Polish displaced persons. We wished this had been done five years earlier.

38

LOTTIE IN AMERICA

OTHER VOICES: Lottie

Many Polish veterans emigrated from England to Canada, Australia, or the United States. A small number went back to their families in western Poland, and some men married English women and stayed in Great Britain. One of my friends, an air force officer, when asked where she was going after the war, replied, "Why, I'm going home, of course." Home for her was a town in China, which was settled by many Polish displaced persons.

By paying for the veterans' transportation to their new homes elsewhere in the world, the English government showed its gratitude to all the Polish soldiers who helped the Allies win the war.

In April of 1950 my father and I booked passage on the Queen Mary for the three-day trip to America. The seas were very turbulent, but I never got seasick. On the ship I roomed with an English girl who was going to the United States for a visit, and we became well acquainted because it was too cold to go outside on deck. Father was afraid of ocean travel and was very uneasy being confined to his cabin.

We docked in New York City, where a girlfriend of mine met us and took us by taxi to Brooklyn, giving a tour of the Big Apple on the way. The next day we taxied to the train station and caught the train to Gary, Indiana.

When Father and I got off the train, our long years of waiting, planning and praying were finally over. I hadn't seen my mother or sisters for about seven years, and my father had said goodbye to his wife and two of his daughters eight years before. My father and I were embraced by Mother, Millie and Lucille one at a time until we all ended up in one big group hug. I don't remember any of us doing a lot of talking. Instead all of us were laughing and crying at the same time, trying to erase the ache of long years of separation. It felt like the past was melting down and our future together was slowly taking its place.

Aunts, uncles and cousins came to welcome us at the station in Gary, but they stayed quietly patient in the background for many minutes while the five of us were getting reacquainted. Then it was their turn to share in the welcoming celebration, and these relatives were silent no more. Everyone talked at once with their introductions and welcome, and I remember getting a lot of attention with my English accent. "Why do you talk so funny?" my younger cousins wanted to know.

Other travelers were staring and smiling with us, joining in our happiness.

That day, Father and I moved our meager belongings into the small apartment with my mother and sisters. We spent the rest of the day and into the night catching up on everyone's activities. Millie and Lucille were very young teenagers when I last saw them, and they were now adults. Because of their common experiences, they were very close. At first I felt like a stranger to them, until we made the adjustment and became a family again.

The next day was reality time. Of course, we all needed to work to help support our household, and I found a job in a factory making gift boxes.

A month after I arrived in the United States, I went with Millie and Stephan to a dance in Chicago, where I met John. We knew each other in England when we were both in the Royal Air Force, but I didn't date him. He was a thin young man during the war, but he gained some weight in America and I thought he looked very handsome.

John was born in the United States, but his mother moved back to Poland with her four children when he was six years old, because, as the oldest sibling in her family, she felt an obligation to take care of her sick mother. English was John's first language, and he learned Polish when he started to school.

After the war started he was drafted into the Polish Air Force. In September of 1939 he and his fellow airmen fled to Romania before the Russians could capture them when Russia invaded Poland. They were forced to give up their arms when they were arrested by the Romanians, who brought them to a prison camp.

The young Polish airmen were frustrated with being confined and idle, and they were anxious to get on with fighting the war. John and dozens of his buddies tried to escape, but they were captured hiding in a ravine near their prison camp. After a second escape attempt also failed, John vowed to his friend, Joe, "We are going to use our heads before we try again."

When the men were first arrested by the Romanians, the officers and enlisted men were confined together. After they were separated into two different living quarters, one soldier acted as a courier between the two groups. John and Joe added their names to his permission paper, and the negligent Romanian guards did not question the extra couriers. The forgers simply strolled out of the prison. They walked a few miles down a road, hiding in the woods whenever they saw anyone.

A rider on a horse came galloping behind them before they could hide themselves. As the horseman approached, Joe and John recognized the uniform of a Romanian officer.

"He has already seen us. It is too late to run now," they decided. "We'll have to brazen it out."

Joe had grown up on a farm and knowing about horses, he calmed the animal by talking to it as he stroked its flank. "What a beautiful animal," he flattered the Romanian.

Perhaps the officer was amused or maybe he was sympathetic to these Polish captives. "OK, you two, I know who you are. Get out of here. Just remember—if anyone asks, you haven't seen me. Now go. Move."

John and Joe could hardly believe their luck, but they didn't waste time thinking about it. They did as ordered. They moved. The two fugitives spent their first night of freedom hiding in a park, covering themselves with newspapers to keep warm. In the morning, a man who hated Germany found them and brought them to a cafeteria and told them, "The owner will feed you."

The sympathizers in the café gave the fugitive airmen a change of clothes and put them on a train to Bucharest where the Polish Embassy outfitted them with fake passports. They were given a different name and identity as civilian students. From there they stopped briefly in Constanta, Romania, on the Black Sea. Then they made their way to Beirut, where the French citizens of Lebanon treated them like royalty, perhaps because John could communicate in fluent French.

These people advised, "You'll need cash to buy food on the French Foreign Legion ship where we're sending you." They gave John enough French francs for their voyage.

On their way to the ship, John and Joe saw some sweet rolls in a bakery window, and the temptation was too much for them. "I'll take two of these please," John ordered.

Perhaps because John assumed all the French-speaking people in Beirut were friendly, he let his guard down.

When they went to pay for the confectionary goodies, which they had already eaten, the shop owner saw an opportunity to cheat the two strangers. He noticed how much money the men carried, and that was what he charged.

"You stupid Pollack," Joe growled at John as soon as they were alone. "Why did you show the baker how much money you had?"

"All right. All right. I was stupid, but we can't go back and argue with him now. That would call too much attention to ourselves," John answered.

"No, we can't. But you'd better figure out a way to get some money when we get to that boat, or we'll starve."

Penniless, they boarded the French Foreign Legion ship. John asked a couple of Legion soldiers, "How can I get some money?"

"You'll have to work for it," one soldier answered.

"Doing what?"

"I have two watches. They start when you tap the glass. Sell these watches for me and you can keep half the money," was the reply.

John set out to hawk the timepieces, but he was having no luck until he approached two Arab Legionnaires.

"Do they work?" he was asked.

"Of course," John said as he tapped the glass.

Money and watches changed hands, and John walked away. He was out of sight of the Arabs when he heard a loud commotion. "Hey, this watch keeps stopping. Where is that asshole who sold it to me? When I find him, I'm going to break his arm and throw him overboard."

Everyone knew the French Foreign Legion accepted soldiers from anywhere in the world with no questions asked. These were tough men, some of whom may have been robbers or murderers, and John didn't want to tangle with any of them. After hearing the Arab's threat, he tried to stay in his cabin, but he did venture out once.

The Legionnaires who first owned the watches saw him and warned, "Oh, oh, here come the Arabs."

Scurrying back to his cabin, John told Joe, "I know they're jerking me around, but I have no choice. We are stuck on this ship until it docks."

"I think those men want you out of sight so the Arabs can't follow your trail back to them," Joe said. "To stay out of trouble, you'll have to do what they want."

When the ship docked in Marseille, France a few days later, Joe and John were the first men to get off, and they didn't look back.

Wanting a way to fight in the war, they volunteered for the army in Finland, but before the arrangements could be completed, these plans fell through. "If we can't go to Finland," Joe decided, "we'll stay in France until we can enlist somewhere."

Not long after this, Germany invaded France, and John said, "We'll have to get out of this country too."

Other Polish fugitives told them, "The British are sending freighters to France to pick up any soldiers from all over the world who want to fight with England."

They boarded a freighter, and by the end of the day, John became a Polish member of the British Royal Air Force.

Day and night for many weeks, all these volunteers were immersed in English language studies. Because English was the only language John spoke until he was six years old, he soon regained his skills. "As of today, John, you are an English teacher," he was informed.

The Poles who spoke good English were given different jobs from the other men, and John instructed the gunners who flew with the pilots. Serving in the Intelligence Unit, he unloaded the cameras from the planes as they landed, and took the film to special rooms where it was analyzed. The men in this room knew at all times how many planes they had and where these machines were. There were also many women working in the Intelligence Unit.

The multinational Royal Air Force had the help of volunteers from Australia, South Africa, Poland, New Zealand, Canada, France, Czechoslovakia, Belgium, Ireland, and the United States. Polish aviators arrived in England in time to be trained before the Battle of Britain began on July 10, 1940, and 139 of these Polish pilots flew with the Royal Air Force to help defeat the German Luftwaffe.

Winston Churchill immortalized the contribution of the Royal Air Force by saying, "Never in the field of human conflict was so much owed by so many to so few."

John learned to respect the British people. While he was at Blackpool, he and several of his buddies lived in a hostel, which was the home of Lilly, their landlady. Her husband was fighting in Burma, and she had a three-year-old son. She cooked and cleaned for her airmen tenants, and for this service she received some money to buy food and supplies, but not much. If civilians in England were asked to take in soldiers, they did so without a second thought. There wasn't enough housing at the military camps.

That first evening we met again, John shared with me all the stories about his experiences during the war, and I also told him what happened to me since I left Poland. Perhaps because we had so much in common, I knew this was a man I wanted to know better.

The following weekend after John and I became reacquainted at that Memorial Day dance, I went to Chicago to see him, and he came to Hammond to see me. We never did get together that day, but we both knew the satisfaction of realizing the other person cared also.

I carried that information in my heart until the next weekend, which we were wise enough to plan. After that, John and I spent every weekend together, and it became more and more difficult to part.

Once John planned to take a bus back to Chicago, but when Stephan drove us to the depot, the last Greyhound had already left. Millie and I decided. "We can put him up at home overnight again."

The Zygmunt family lived in an apartment with two small bedrooms, a tiny living room, a kitchen and one bath. Father and Mother were asleep in their bedroom. I gave John the couch where I usually slept, and with sheets, a pillow and a blanket, he soon settled into his space.

I shared Millie and Lucille's bed. We were now adults with the same sleeping arrangements we had as young children. All of our lives we had lived in tight spaces, and because no one was bothered by the close quarters, we all managed to fall asleep that night, but not for long. A loud CRA-ACK brought our bed down with a CRA-ASH. The whole household now awakened to find arms, sheets, pillows, legs and splintered wood entangled on the floor.

"I can see no one is hurt," quipped Father, "since you are all laughing."

Millie and Lucille were asking each other, "Why did we buy such a cheap bed when we came to America?"

"Because you didn't have much money," my parents answered in unison.

There was no way to repair the bed that night. John carried the splintered bed frame to one side, and my sisters and I pushed the mattress against the wall and tucked in enough sheets and blankets. Between the laughing and the uncomfortable sleeping positions, no one got much rest, but we were young.

Several times John came to Hammond on the South Shore Railroad and he stayed with me so long that he missed his transportation back to Chicago. "Stephan, will you drive me back to Chicago please?" John asked each time.

Millie and Stephan would have to help us again. Neither John nor I owned a car, and it was very inconvenient to date by train.

After a few more weekends when we wasted hours in travel instead of being together, John announced, "We're both adults who've fought in a war. We're not young kids anymore. We don't want to wait; let's get married now. I love you. You will make me the happiest man in the world if you will do me the honor of becoming my wife?"

There was no question in my mind. "Of course, I'll marry you. I want to spend the rest of my life with you,"

We both agreed, "We want to get married right away."

"Stephan won't miss his late night chauffeuring trips to Chicago," we both laughed.

Our families greeted our happy news with many smiles and congratulations. They all wanted the best for us.

My future father-in-law met our engagement announcement with one of his own. "I have missed all other family occasions being separated from my family for 25 years. I want this to be a special wedding."

He chose to give us a big wedding in Chicago, for which he made all the arrangements. He invited 500 people, most of whom were friends of his. This was not a popular decision with my family and friends in Hammond, but all I could say was, "My father-in-law is planning and paying for our reception, and he is making the decisions."

John was 34 and I was 26 years old when we married in 1950. I moved to Chicago to be with my new husband, where I worked in a factory making fruit jar lids, and John worked as a machinist.

We met again on Memorial Day, 1950, and October 7 of that same year we became husband and wife.

39

WALTER IN AMERICA

Walter Zygmunt saved and worked hard all of his life, and he owned a farm which supported a family of six. He served in the military service of his country four times for a total of about eight years, and he arrived in America almost naked. He owned no possessions except one suitcase of clothes. At 52 years of age, he had no net worth. He was called a displaced person, a *wygnaniec* in the Polish language. What he did have was great pride in being Polish, and after he came to the United States, he quickly became very proud to be an American.

When he arrived, his three daughters were well into their twenties. He decided my mother had done a good job in raising us for the last eight years. "I won't start handing down fatherly advice or suggestions now. Make your own bed. Just remember—you'll have to lie in it," he told us.

Lottie and my father moved into the small two-bedroom apartment my mother rented with Lucille and me.

Walter relaxed around the house for a whole 18 hours before he was hired at General American. Outdoors in all kinds of weather, rain or shine, hot or cold, he took apart railroad cars using a large sledge hammer. The job was paid by piece work, and if he didn't work hard, he wouldn't earn much. He wouldn't ever call in sick, and fortunately he was healthy and still able to do this grueling labor. All of us shared the chores around the apartment, but my parents did the cooking. They were both very neat around the kitchen, and their daughters were too messy. "It's easier for us to do the cooking than to teach you. Anyway, you have your jobs, and we want you to have a good time with your friends," was their reasoning.

My two sisters and I were again sharing a tiny bedroom just as we did back in Poland. It was so crowded that Lottie asked, "Is it OK if I sleep on the couch?"

Lucille and I answered in unison, "Yes, of course."

There was not enough room for five adults in the small two-bedroom apartment, but my sisters soon solved that problem by getting married.

At a dance in Chicago, Lottie became reacquainted with John, who was also in the air force in England. He started coming to Hammond to spend weekends with us, and now we were really crowded. On October 7 of 1950, she married him and moved to Chicago.

"I am so happy for you," I told Lottie. I was also glad for the extra bedroom and closet space Lucille and I now shared, but I knew I would miss my sister now that we were reacquainted.

My younger sister, Lucille, met a man at a dance at the Polish Veteran's Hall. She dated him for a year or so before they married in 1952.

About a week after we came to America, we signed the first papers to become citizens, and in

September of 1953 Mother, Lucille and I, with about ten other people, went to the post office on State Street in Hammond for the ceremony, which made us citizens of the United States. We were questioned by a judge, and he wrote down our answers. Then there was an impressive ceremony. When we became citizens, it was one of the happiest days of our lives. We had no country after Poland was taken over by the Russians. We couldn't go back there, because we didn't want to live in Russia or any other Communist country. United States citizenship gave us the homeland we love now. We are proud to be Americans.

American citizenship is equal to a million dollars—no, a whole lot more. You can't buy anything with more value than this. It's worth everything to have citizenship papers of the United States. It stands for freedom.

When they play The Star Spangled Banner or America, I always cry.

Also in 1953, my parents bought a small, two-bedroom house on Wabash Avenue in Hammond, and I was able to lend them $2000 for part of the down payment. Thirteen years after their farm in Poland was stolen, Walter and Stephanie became proud homeowners again, this time in the United States. America is the land of opportunity.

40

OUR ENGAGEMENT

My date with Stephan to Danceland on Valentine's Day started our courtship. We were soul mates who liked to do the same things. We saw every movie that came out, and when we went to a dinner dance, we barely ate our food. Our friends would buy a bottle and Stephan and I might have one drink, but mostly we were on the dance floor.

We dated for five years, but sometimes we broke up for a whole weekend or so. Once Stephan showed me photos of girls he knew in England, and maybe I thought he sounded a little too proud of those pictures. I snapped, "I don't think they're THAT good looking."

There probably wasn't anything he could say to repair the damage after that, but he tried. "Oh no, I just mean I had fun with them."

"Oh, and you don't have a good time with me?"

When he called the next day, neither of us mentioned English girls or fun with any other partners. He said, "Would you like to go to the movies?" And all was well between us.

We might have a fight about some small thing and break up, but neither of us dated anyone else and we always got back together again right away. Perhaps he wanted me to do something I didn't want to do, and I might show my temper.

Sometimes I would admit the fight was my fault, and on other occasions he called me first.

After we dated for four years, I was given the opportunity to go to a five-week Polish National Alliance convention and workshop in Pennsylvania, where I lived in a large college dorm without a telephone. Stephan couldn't call me, but I phoned him every few days, admitting, "I'm so lonely for you."

"How do you know?" he asked.

"Because I think about you every few minutes all day long," I confessed.

Another man drove all the way to Pennsylvania to ask me to marry him, but I didn't even hesitate. My "no" answer sent him driving all the way back from Pennsylvania.

When I arrived back in Hammond after five weeks, I knew I needed to be with this man named Stephan. If he wanted me, I certainly wanted him.

Stephan didn't have to wait for me to come home to realize there was a big change in my attitude. He could tell I was ready for a commitment. On my 28th birthday, we were invited to the wedding of one of my friends from Tengeru Camp in Africa. Stephan was driving me and my parents to Chicago for the reception.

I met Stephan before my dad came to this country, but my father loved him right away too. They also had much in common, like fighting with the same unit in the same battles in Italy during World War II. They were both soldiers in the battle of Monte Cassino.

I was still getting dressed when Stephan came a little early. In an old-fashioned way, he kissed my mother's cheek and shook my father's hand. "Sir, I love your daughter, and I want to spend the rest of my life with her. May I have her hand in marriage?"

"You certainly do have my blessing," my father agreed.

When I came into the kitchen, Stephan opened a small box and put a ring on my finger. He said, "I love you and I want you to wear this diamond as a symbol of my feelings for you. Will you marry me?"

Without a second thought, I said, "Of course I'll marry you, because I love you too."

The engagement ring circled around a large diamond, a whole carat. Later on our wedding day, Stephan admitted to me, "I was so confident that I paid for your wedding ring and my wedding ring at the same time as I bought your engagement ring."

At the reception of my friend from Camp Tengeru, I showed her my new engagement ring. She smiled, "Wonderful. Now you will be as happy as I am today."

Stephan was introduced to a lot of people that night, and he received almost as many congratulations as the groom. And, oh yes, the sparkle in my eyes was brighter then the shine of my new diamond.

41

DANCE SCHOOL

I am a member of Lodge 3095, Council 49, of the Polish National Alliance in Hammond. In 1953, they owned a large college in Cambridge Springs, Pennsylvania.

Every year this alliance organized classes for Polish youth at their college. They taught dancing, exercising, singing, camping, and the Polish and English languages. It was also like a finishing school, in that the delegates learned how to be young ladies and gentlemen.

Since I was able to get a five-week sabbatical from my job, I was selected, at the age of 27, to attend this seminar. "You are expected to go back to your local lodges and councils to teach others what you have learned," they told all the delegates.

A friend and I took a train from Chicago. At the college, we lived in rustic dorm rooms that had a narrow bed and a desk and not much else, but we were kept so busy we didn't have much time to notice our accommodations.

In the morning we got up at 6:00 to exercise by running two miles. Then we sang the Polish Morning Song and raised the Polish flag. We were given uniforms and special hats, all to give us a sense of belonging and solidarity. This worked for me, because I made some new friends. I went to all the classes they offered except the Polish lessons. Since that is my first language, I knew I could have taught that course. The camp supervisor asked, "Why aren't you studying Polish?" I told her the truth, "I need the English instruction more." I tried to absorb as much from those classes as I could. Lucille and I took an English-as-a-Second-Language course when we first came to this country, but we couldn't afford the lessons for as long as we needed to go.

When I returned home, I organized two dance classes for children from the ages of three to sixteen. One group met on Saturday morning in north Hammond, and the other met in the eastern part of town on Wednesday evening. The kids were mostly very attentive and cooperative. At times I would have to show them each step, sometimes taking a leg and pushing it in the right direction.

They learned the *krakowiak, polonez, kujawiak, polka* and *trojak.* Of all the dances, the polka is the most flexible, because you can dance anyway you want as long as you keep the rhythm and the step. You can turn around or you can jump. Everyone dances the polka in a different way, and as long as you agree with your partner, whatever you do is all right.

The lessons lasted for two hours, after which I was exhausted. I told my mother, "I have learned a new appreciation for teachers with large classes. They work very hard." For this two-hour dance instruction, I was paid $5.00. This was the total sum—not $5.00 from each child. I taught these classes twice a week for two years.

I still meet some of the kids I taught 50 years ago. Of course, I do not recognize them because they are much older now, but they still know me. It is a good feeling when someone I meet says, "Hello, Millie. You taught me to polka a half century ago."

42

WEDDING SHOWERS

In my dresser drawer at home is a 53-year-old guest list recording the gifts everyone brought to our wedding showers. These friends gave us every small electric appliance we wanted, plus sheets and towels, silverware, dishes and money. We now owned everything we would need to set up housekeeping.

Big wedding showers are the tradition in the Polish-American community, and when Stephan's aunt gave a party for us, she invited many of her club, church and neighborhood friends. I still have a pressed white orchid my fiancé brought me for that occasion. My mother also gave a shower for us at her house.

Six years before, we landed in America with nothing except a big debt. Now I had everything, and I'm not talking about possessions.

43

OUR WEDDING

Saturday, May 8, 1954, dawned sunny and cool. I was already walking on air when I woke up, because I was getting the man I wanted. My memories of our wedding day are mostly about Stephan and me and what we did together. I was barely aware of other people. I was so far up in the clouds that the next thing I remember, we were at the church.

As my father was escorting me, wearing my white dress and veil, down the long aisle of St. Casimir's Church, I could not see Stephan. I could see the best man and groomsmen, but my husband-to-be was not there. For a minute I thought he got cold feet and decided to escape to Mexico, but actually he was shorter than the other two men and was hidden behind them. When I saw him, I whispered to my father, "He is so handsome in his tuxedo."

After the 10:00 a.m. ceremony, our guests met us at the Polish Veteran's Hall where there was a hot lunch of soup, chicken, beef, sauerkraut and chop suey. Yes, chop suey. When we hired the cook, she gave us a list of all the food we should have on hand at the hall. She asked for whole chickens, and she used all the parts of the chicken, including the gizzard and liver to make the chop suey.

Photo #7

Millie and Stephan - 1954

After lunch our guests were on their own for the afternoon, and Stephan and I went home to rest up for the 6:00 reception that evening. I remember a lot more about those few hours, but that is all I'm going to tell you, except to say, "We didn't get a lot of rest."

I think it showered that afternoon because some ladies later told us. "Rain on your wedding day means good luck."

While our guests enjoyed an open bar that evening, we stood at a reception line with my parents, Stephan's aunt and uncle, and our attendants. Lucille was my matron of honor. Our other attendants were friends from the neighborhood or work, while the children of Stephan's cousin were flower girl and ring bearer.

After everyone was seated at their tables, all of us were formally introduced. Stephan's best man, a long-standing friend from Russia and the army, toasted us by saying, "May you have good health and dozens of children."

The President of the United States could have walked in the door and I wouldn't have noticed—I was so focused on Stephan. I think we went from table to table talking to everyone, "How was your dinner?" "The bar is open all evening." Even though Polish people don't have to be told to have fun at a party, we also said, "Have a good time."

When the band started, the bride and groom enjoyed their first waltz together as man and wife. Then I danced with my father, and my husband and his Aunt Marie were partners.

After the introductory dances, I was still floating in a dream world as Stephan and I danced the night away.

A tradition at Polish weddings was for the bride to sit on the groom's lap while the bridesmaids take off her veil and put on her apron. I threw my bouquet to the eligible ladies, and Stephan took the garter off my thigh and threw it to the bachelors.

Although our guests stayed until 2:00 or 3:00 a.m., the grand marshal signaled the official end of the reception at 11:00 p.m., which meant the bride and groom were free to leave. The tradition at that time called for the groom to carry the bride away from their reception hall. This signified that she was now his woman, and his alone. I only weighed 118 pounds, but Stephan was not a large man. He staggered a bit, and I thought he was going to drop me. I believe there is a good reason this custom is no longer practiced at weddings.

We slept at my parent's house that night, where we would be starting our married life.

Sunday morning was *poprawiny*, a tradition brought from Poland, where the marriage celebrations lasted for two or three days. In the United States *poprawiny* is just the morning after the reception, and it includes the noon lunch of food left over from the wedding dinner.

Stephan's aunt had a friend who owned a grocery store. That good lady gave us all the food from our cook's list and charged us only $64 for lunch and dinner for 150 guests, plus 25 people for *poprawiny*.

We were amazed at the generosity of some of our friends. Of course, not all the guests could afford to be that giving, but we didn't care what their presents were. We wanted everyone to come to our wedding and be happy with us.

On Monday morning Stephan and I drove to Niagara Falls and Montreal, Canada, in his shiny new four-door Chevy. Stephan had earned two weeks of paid vacation, and he wanted to spend that much time on our honeymoon. I was entitled to only one week of vacation, and because I didn't want to lose any money, he gave in and our wedding trip lasted just one week.

Money was too important to me because I couldn't get past the insecurity of being poor and hungry for so long. I also thought we would have 50 years of happiness together.

I was stupid.

44

THE HOUSE THAT STEPHEN BUILT

I discovered that Stephan was whole and healthy except for the hole in his hip and the shrapnel in his back.

Was he good in bed? Yes, he was very good. He was patient, and because he knew women needed more time, he waited for me. He slowed down so I could catch up. I don't know how other men are, but I think that's very important.

After our wedding, we moved in with my parents where we lived rent free. I had loaned them $2000 at no interest to buy their house, which they paid back in installments.

When I married Stephan, I was working, of course. I was so happy married to him because he was so thoughtful. I assumed every woman lived with a good mate, but I found out later that not all men are faithful and true. He was a perfect husband—the best man I ever knew.

When we disagreed about something, Stephan never went to bed without making up. If he had a bad day at work, he never brought those troubles home.

I couldn't believe the miracle of this marriage to Stephan could happen to me. Sometimes I thought my dad loved him more than he loved me or my sisters. "I believe Stephan became the son you never had," I told my father. My husband was good to my parents; he listened when they spoke to him. My dad treasured him, and my mother worshipped him.

Stephan was very handy and he would help his uncle or my dad around the house. There was almost nothing he couldn't fix, but if he couldn't repair it, he knew where to go. He helped anyone who called. One cold morning at 2:00 a.m., an old lady called Stephan to say, "There is no heat at my home."

He went to her house and patched up her heater so it would work for awhile, after which he went to work at his job. Two days later the woman owned a new furnace which he ordered and installed with his free labor.

He did all of this while he worked a full-time job. We were both working, and we both saved, saved, saved. We learned that trait from our upbringings.

Some nosy busybody said at our wedding, "Millie will be the boss because Stephan is so quiet," but it wasn't like that at all. I bought every dress on condition that I could return it to the store if my husband didn't like it.

We made all important decisions together. Stephan wanted to build a new house for us. "I don't want to move that far away from my parents," I protested.

"Let's make a list of all the good reasons for building our own house, and another list for all the negative things," he suggested.

Moving away from my parents was the only bad reason, but it was a good one also, because we would have more privacy. There were about 20 things we would gain from a new house, starting with, "We'll have more room," "It's a good investment," and "We can start a family."

Both of us said, "Let's build." We made the decision together for our future.

Stephan showed me the blueprints, of which I understood nothing. He told me, "Don't worry about it because I know what I'm doing." I trusted him.

By building our one-story castle, Stephan was enjoying himself. Those first two years of our marriage, he constructed our house with very little help. My father and a couple of cousins would work with him when they could, and Stephan hired someone to pour the cement basement floor and to plaster the walls. He did all the carpentry, including the framing. The plumbing and electricity, the floors and cabinets, he did himself. He put up the cement block foundation and the brick on the outside of our home. The Hammond City Inspector checked each job along the way, and my husband was such a competent builder that his work passed every inspection.

Stephan bought materials as he needed them, and he made payments monthly as he went along. If he needed a tool he used every day, he bought it, but he didn't waste money on equipment that just sat around. If he needed something for just a few days, he would rent it.

Neither of us spent money foolishly, and we paid off our whole mortgage in the two years after Stephan built the house. We didn't have any money worries.

That wasn't the only reason I was so happy being married to Stephan. He was so thoughtful. If he was going to be just ten minutes late, he would call me. He helped around the house; he took care of all the bills. Before I started driving a car, he called after work to see if I needed anything from the grocery store. Throughout our marriage, he remembered every birthday and anniversary with bouquets of roses. Often he brought a nosegay of cut flowers—just because. If Stephan didn't have a compliment to give someone, he didn't say anything at all. He never complained about other people. He didn't drink much, and he didn't have any vices except smoking. I told my mother, "I have a perfect husband."

However, after our marriage I started losing weight because I wasn't eating properly. My doctor prescribed various things like wine before dinner, but I couldn't gain weight. After about six months, the doctor told me, "Stop coming. I can't think of anything else to try."

I was working too hard, but I think I felt guilty for being so happy. Never before had my life been so wonderful. Stephan was so good to me that I didn't know how to handle it. Every day I hurried home from work so I could see him again. I finally must have decided, "I deserve to have these feelings," because after about a year of marriage, I began to relax and gain back the weight I'd lost.

My husband and I wanted to start a family and when nothing was happening, our doctor checked both of us and told us, "You are both healthy. Relax. Take it easy. Enjoy yourself with the plans

Photo #8

The house Stephan built

for your new home."

We decided to take his advice. We enjoyed every minute of our house construction. Our castle was not large, but it was just right for us. The front door opened directly into our carpeted 18 x 22 foot living room. The kitchen featured a handy U-shaped working area with birch cabinets and stainless steel built-in appliances. There was a refrigerator with a large freezer on the bottom, and we said, "We'll never go hungry again."

The electric stove top and oven were also built in. Very important to us was our drop-leaf table with three leaves, which opened large enough to seat 14 people, because we wanted to be able to serve dinners to our whole families.

There were two bedrooms. We had a bathroom upstairs and one in the basement. Wood paneling, the latest thing, covered the downstairs recreation room walls, and Stephan built artificial windows with a light that shone on a beautiful mural. Space was set aside for a bar, but he didn't put it in right away. He said, "This will be my project for next winter."

A small basement refrigerator and stove were handy for our many large family parties.

Our castle was so beautiful that we were never going to move again.

45

LOTTIE IN CALIFORNIA

OTHER VOICES: Lottie

In 1955, John developed a bad knee which was so swollen and painful he couldn't walk. The doctor told us, "He cannot continue to work as a machinist. He needs a drier and warmer climate like Arizona."

We didn't know anyone in Arizona, but John's friend lived in California. Both of our mothers didn't want us to leave. "We were separated from our families during the war and we don't want you to move away from us again," they both pleaded.

"Moving to California is important for John's health, and we are going," we decided.

It took us a week to drive out west in our brand new Chevrolet. We paid $1700 for that car, which was a lot of money in 1955.

In California John found a job at Rockwell International making gyroscopes for space travel. The air in his workroom needed to be very clean, with the result that his health improved after our move. This turned out to be a very good job.

After a few years our families agreed, "You did the right thing."

Many decades after we moved to California, we received a letter from Lillie, John's landlady in England during the war.

Dear John and Lottie,

My lady friend and I would like to plan a holiday to the United States this summer. Do you think we might stay with you for a few days while we are in California?

Your friend and landlady, Lilly

John was excited about seeing Lilly again and entertaining her at our home. He replied by return mail.

Dear Lilly,

It would be our pleasure to welcome you and your friend to our home. Don't plan to stay a few days. Come for a month. There is a lot to see in California. Just let us know when and where you will be arriving.

Sincerely,
Your friends, John and Lottie

Lilly stayed for a month. "I have never had such a wonderful holiday," she exclaimed. "You took us to Mexico, to the movie studios and to Disneyland. We would like to give you something for your hospitality."

John would have nothing to do with her money. "I can never repay you for your kindnesses to me and my fellow airmen during the war. I've enjoyed reliving our good memories of you and the English people. It's been our pleasure to entertain you."

Lilly cried when she left our home.

And she wasn't the only one.

46

MIRACLES

Early in 1956, Stephan picked me up from my job and we went right out to our new house, which was finished except for the painting. We planned to start decorating that evening. He had just opened the paint can when I became so nauseous from the fumes that I started throwing up.

"Did you eat something that didn't agree with you?" Stephan asked.

"No, I didn't," was my answer.

"Then you must be catching the flu, Millie," Stephan decided. "I think you should stay home for a day or two until you get over it."

I disagreed. "I don't want to get over it."

"Of course you want to get over it."

"No, I don't."

He looked at me, and after a moment or two, he said, "You're smiling."

"Yes, I'm smiling."

"You're going to have a baby, aren't you?"

"Yes," I agreed. "I think I'm going to have a baby."

Stephan started waltzing around the room. He bowed to me. "May I have this dance?" he asked.

"No," I smiled while standing in front of the fresh air at an open window.

My answer didn't stop Stephan. He kept whirling around the room by himself, folding his arms around an imaginary lady.

"Who is your partner?" I asked.

"My daughter. We're waltzing at her wedding."

"What if he's a boy?" I wanted to know.

"Then you dance with him," he said as he continued to lead his daughter in the three-quarter rhythm. "I'm happy with her."

I was just as happy breathing the fresh air and watching my husband and his imaginary daughter. He came to my side, "The doctor was right, wasn't he?"

We had been trying to become parents for a long time. Both of us went to the doctor because we were concerned that being undernourished for so many years had damaged something important. After all of our test results came in, the doctor said, "You are both healthy, and there is nothing wrong with either of you. You are trying too hard. Relax. Take it easy. Stop thinking so much."

"Yes," I agreed with my husband. "The doctor was right. I got pregnant when we stopped trying. I am going to have a baby."

Of course, Stephan now decided, "I will do all the painting at our house,"

But no more work got done that evening. It was a night for celebrating, and Stephan wanted to give me a big kiss, but my sour breath convinced him to settle for a quick peck on my cheek. We started to think about names we liked for our baby girl or boy, and we talked about what he or she might want to do later in his or her life. We wondered how many grandchildren we might have some day.

During the next few weeks, Stephan became anxious about me and our unborn baby. At my first appointment with the doctor who would be monitoring my pregnancy, I said, "Doctor, my husband is worried about our baby."

"Mrs. Rytel, why is your husband concerned?"

"You don't understand. We have bad things in our past."

"What don't I understand? Tell me."

"We were both overworked and starving in a Siberian labor camp during World War II," I blurted out.

"For how long?"

"For a couple of years."

"My dear Mrs. Rytel, the human body can withstand a lot of abuse. Your job now is to get plenty of rest, some exercise and healthy foods. Will you do that?"

"Yes, I will, but . . ."

"Mrs. Rytel, I will watch out for your baby. That's my job, and I do it well. Now we will both attend to the work we do best. Is that a deal?" he extended his hand.

"Yes, doctor," I smiled as I shook his hand.

At this time, we were still living with my parents. We kept the secret of my pregnancy from our families for about two more months. That wasn't as difficult as it seems, because I didn't have morning sickness. I worked the early shift at my job and when I came home, my mother's dinner was ready for us, so I didn't have to cook. At night I told everyone, "I'm tired from my job, and I'm going to bed."

Stephan was worried about me and fussed over me, but not in front of my parents, and they were not suspicious.

When we finally told my parents, they said, "It's about time." They were proud that they were going to be grandparents for the second time. My mother said what mothers say, "How do you feel?" "Is everything OK?" "Have you been to a doctor?" "Are you doing what he says?" "Are you sure you should be working?"

My husband's Aunt Marie asked, "Do you need any help with furnishing the baby's room?"

When I replied, "I haven't thought about that room yet," she gave me her grandchildrens' baby bed.

On April 10, 1956, we moved our furniture into our immaculate new house, including the bedroom set I bought before I was married. Our home had no driveway or sidewalks yet, but the house was beautifully constructed and decorated. We enjoyed privacy for the first time in our married life.

Late in the month of October in 1956, I again became ill, this time with stomach pains. "Oh, honey, is your heartburn acting up again? Did you take your medicine?" Stephan wanted to know.

"No, I haven't taken my medicine, and yes, my heart is talking to me."

"I'll get your heartburn medication," my husband said as he rose from his chair.

"Stephan, I don't want my medicine. I want my suitcase."

"Oh, my goodness," he exclaimed. "The baby is coming."

We went to the hospital as fast as Stephan could drive. While he filled out the admitting papers, the nurses took me away to the labor room. They measured my pains for a few hours until the baby's birth was near.

In those days, husbands were kept out of delivery rooms, and Stephan began pacing the waiting area and the hospital corridors with the other fathers-to-be. An hour later, the doctor came out and said, "Mr. Rytel, your wife is doing just fine, and you have a healthy eight-pound, ten-ounce baby girl."

She was perfect, and we named her Christine.

When our new daughter and I were discharged from the hospital, Stephan took us home. A few weeks later, Chris became sick. After a feeding she would start shaking and screaming in pain, and she turned blue with convulsions. The doctor came to our house, but he couldn't figure out what was wrong with her. He put her in the hospital so he could take some tests, and when he changed her milk, she was immediately OK. She was simply allergic to her first formula.

Our second daughter, Liz, was born five years later on September 17, 1961. She weighed five pounds, twelve ounces, and she was also perfect.

Just perfect.

Our babies were indeed—miracles.

47

LEARNING TO DRIVE

One day I was walking the seven blocks to our church, where I went three times a week for evening services. An old lady driving about five or ten miles per hour went past me.

I asked myself, "What's wrong with me? If she can drive, I can drive. I have to learn. I'm not that old and I'm not that stupid."

My husband agreed, "You can learn to drive without taking lessons, because I'll teach you." So he took me to Wolf Lake in Hammond where the large paved area is ideal for practicing drivers. Stephan told me about the gear shift lever. He explained the gas, temperature, and oil pressure gauges. He showed me the lights and the emergency brake.

Only then did he give me the keys, and I put the car in gear and stepped on the gas pedal.

Maybe I didn't stop soon enough as I was driving toward the lake. Stephan yelled at me. "What's wrong with you? You almost drove the car into the lake."

Maybe I stepped on the gas and the brake at the same time. He shouted, "You're ruining the engine."

I put the transmission in Park, opened the door and got out of the car. With hands on my hips, I told Stephan, "You're not going to yell at me." I started walking to our house, which was about two or three miles from Wolf Lake. He drove behind me and tried to pick me up, but I would NOT get in the car. I stomped home, steaming all the way.

Several months later I was at a party and some lady told me, "There is an adult driving course at Purdue University that's supposed to be good."

I lived only one block away, so the next Monday I registered and paid my $25 fee for six sessions, but I didn't tell my husband, and the next Wednesday I started the class. By the second lesson, we all took our turn behind the wheel in the driver training car lent to the school by a car dealership.

After about two lessons I finally told my husband what I was doing. He said, "I would have taught you how to drive."

On the third lesson the instructor, meeting with me and a younger girl, announced, "OK, now we're going to South Bend. Mrs. Rytel, you get behind the wheel. Miss Wilson, you will be driving back to Hammond."

South Bend was about 50 miles away, and it was 6:00 in the evening when we started. The instructor sat next to me, but he didn't have dual controls or a brake or any way to control the car if I made a mistake. The first time I drove on a regular street, I was speeding in rush hour traffic down Interstate 80/94, one of the busiest expressways in the country. I was keeping up with the traffic, chasing the trucks at 75 miles per hour.

My instructor said, "You're going to kill us all." But somehow I made it to South Bend, and we were all still alive. The teacher breathed more easily, and I collapsed in the back seat as the younger girl drove back to Hammond. She had previous driving experience, and the traffic was lighter on our return trip.

Meanwhile Stephan was at home with the children, and by 8:00 p.m. he got very worried when it started raining, and the roads became slippery. My husband, panicking because he knew what a poor driver I was, packed up our two children, and they sat for hours in the armory waiting for me to come back. When we finally came in later that night, he was very relieved.

He said, "I've gotten my wife back in one piece." And we both laughed as he added, "I would have taught you how to drive."

When I got my driver's license, I thought, "Now I am a true American. I'm independent and free as a bird. America belongs to me."

48

SETTLING INTO MARRIED LIFE

We were settling into married life, but Stephan had a major problem. He hadn't talked to his mother and father in Poland for 15 years. He didn't like being estranged from his parents, even though it was for their own protection because he was afraid they would be persecuted if their son contacted them from America.

Finally Stephan decided he would become his own cousin. He wrote to his parents as their nephew.

Dear Aunt Sophie and Uncle Frank,

You will be surprised to get a letter from your nephew. Do you remember when I stayed with Stephan at your house when I was a little boy, and you taught me how to milk a cow? I liked to squirt the milk at the cat, didn't I? You told me to stop that.

I am married now to Millie and we have a daughter named Christine. We live in a new house in America. Please write to us.

Love, Your nephew, Harry

His parents figured out what Stephan was doing from his clues about his childhood, and they began a correspondence with their "nephew." After awhile, still pretending to be nephew and niece, we sent a visa for his mother to come and visit us in the United States. She stayed for six months, and she was so impressed with America that she wanted to live here.

I remember the first time we took her to a grocery store. She started screaming in Polish, "My God, in the wintertime you've got bananas and oranges. Where are they coming from?"

She touched them to be sure they were real, because in Communist Poland they often carved fruits and vegetables from wood and painted them to look real.

In Poland 40 years ago, they thought all Americans were rich and the money just came pouring in by itself. They thought the streets were paved with gold. Stephan's mother was surprised to see how hard her son worked.

We invited both of Stephan's parents to come to America and live with us. His mother wanted to stay permanently, but her husband didn't want to go to the United States. He said, "I have fought for Poland and I want to die in my own country." Another reason they wouldn't come was because they thought they would be a burden to Stephan and he would have to work that much harder to support two more people. So his mother went back to their farm to be with her husband and take care of him.

Stephan went to Poland twice to visit his parents and, of course, he pretended to be their nephew. The first time he stayed for his two-week vacation, but later he had a sabbatical from work for six weeks, so that time he spent helping his parents on their farm. He came back in September right before my parents' 50th anniversary celebration.

Our families were important to both of us, and when we entertained in our new home, it was usually for my family or Stephan's. I had a lot of parties there. We enjoyed that house, and Stephan was always improving it. He offered to build another larger house for me, but I didn't want to move any farther from my parents.

Instead he bought a large lot in Schererville where he built a duplex which we rented out. He said, "In the future that area will be subdivided, and we will make a lot of money." It was Stephan's hobby to buy land and build on it. He also bought a duplex in the Woodmar section of Hammond. All the property was soon paid off. When I asked why he wanted to work so hard, he answered, "I'm investing in our future."

He also invested a lot of energy in his job. Stephan was such a devoted worker, and he never took time off from work. When he was sick, he went to work anyway. He missed just one day in 23 years on the job, and that was when he was running a very high fever.

Although he was demanding on himself, he always made me take it easy when I wasn't feeling well. When the children were little, he would tell me, "Don't be too fussy with the housekeeping. Relax and enjoy the kids."

Even though he wanted me not to work as hard as he did, I still wanted to help him. When we were first married and I was still working, we sent his work clothes to the laundry. I bought a new Whirlpool washer and dryer with money I earned running the dance schools. I kept that washer for 35 years, because I was very careful not to overload it or put in too much detergent.

At one point Stephan bought another Whirlpool machine for me, and we kept the old washer for his dirty work clothes. Sometimes the pants and shirts would be full of hanging grease, but if I soaked his clothes in a special solution before washing them, I could get the oily dirt out and save the $4 for each article it would cost at the cleaners. We counted every dollar.

Another wifely duty I had was making his lunch every day. "Your ham and salami sandwiches are so good that the other men want me to share my lunch," he said. At least that's what he told me. When we were first married, I couldn't cook. My parents were both professional cooks, but they didn't teach any of their daughters. After all of us got to America, we were so busy working long shifts and overtime that there simply wasn't time for learning our way around a kitchen. Stephan had worked with his aunt in her grocery and delicatessen, and she gave him recipes and taught him how to prepare them. When we moved into our new home, Stephan gave me cooking lessons.

Both of us could have used some lessons in English, because neither of us spoke the American language very well.

It was easier for us to speak Polish at home with our children when they were little, but we agreed, "We need to use more English for our daughters' sakes." We decided to improve our English by talking with our American friends, but to tell you the truth, we learned more from our children after they went to school.

When Chris first started in kindergarten, she understood English but couldn't speak that language at all. I went to the school and asked her teacher, "Does Chris have a problem?"

The teacher replied, "No, she will learn English very fast."

In two weeks Chris spoke English all the time. She picked it up at school and from her friends as they played, and Stephan and I learned from our daughter.

I didn't go back to work until Liz, my second daughter, was eight years old. I filled out an application for a job in housekeeping at the Whiting Clinic across the street from where we lived, and two days later they hired me. I couldn't work as a registered nurse, licensed practical nurse, or even a nurse's aide, because the United States would not accept my African diploma.

When I told my husband, "I have a new job," I knew from the expression on his face that my working didn't make him happy.

On my first payday I wanted to take my family out to eat, but Stephan put his foot down, "No, I won't go. Your check is for you to spend on yourself." He wouldn't even look at the amount.

My shift was from 4:00 in the evening until 2:00 a.m. The clinic was open all night, and on the evenings I worked, Stephan would read a story to Liz, our youngest, as he tucked her into bed. He was very strict with our children, but he was loving, just as my father had been with his three daughters.

Stephan was offered a job managing a large condo complex nearby, where he could use all his plumbing, carpentry and electricity skills. He could fix anything. The job paid well in salary and benefits. "I must work two more years at Inland Steel until I can get a pension," he decided, "and after that I'll quit and find an easier, cleaner job."

He had a contractor's license and he wanted to remodel run-down homes on his day off.

"I want my husband to be home with me and our daughters. We'll never see you if you work seven days a week," I protested.

He agreed.

Instead he stayed busy doing projects at home. Stephan had a big workbench with all the tools. He wanted to make wooden furniture. He built a beautiful china cabinet with mirrors and delicate doors for in our dining room.

We didn't work all the time; we had fun too. We owned a cottage in Winnemac, Indiana, on the Tippecanoe River, which we used for recreation. We loved to stop for a turkey dinner at the Strongbow Inn in Valparaiso on the way home from our cabin. Stephan's shift at that time was to work five days through the weekend, and then he was off on two weekdays.

Sometimes I couldn't go to Tippecanoe with the family because I was working. On those days, Stephan would always stop off to buy flowers to give me when I got home.

"Millie, I don't like to see you working so hard. I want you to quit," he said many times.

I decided to try for a compromise. "All right, Stephan, let me work through this next winter, and then we can talk about my quitting next spring."

Stephan agreed, and we took a break from discussing our jobs.

49

50TH ANNIVERSARY PARTY

1921 – 1971

SURPRISE
You are cordially invited to the
50th Anniversary celebration honoring
Stephanie and Walter Zygmunt
on Saturday, September 4

Mass at 5:00 p.m.
Saint Casimir's Catholic Church
4340 Johnson Street, Hammond, Indiana

Dinner at 6:00 p.m.
Polish Veteran's Hall, Hammond, Indiana
Dancing 8:00 until?

Given by their daughters: Please reply to:
Lottie Koziel   Millie Rytel
Millie Rytel   555 Schneider Av.
LucilleKrupa   Hammond, Indiana

My sisters and I planned a surprise 50th anniversary party for our parents. When my phone rang the day before the party, I knew the cat was out of the bag the minute I heard my mother's voice asking, "What's going on, Millie?"

"What do you mean?" I stalled.

My mother continued, "My neighbor just told me we're having an anniversary party."

I couldn't think of anything to say except to tell the truth. "Well, Mother, you know your beige dress with the golden threads—the one we insisted you buy a few weeks ago? Well, you are wearing it tomorrow," I told her.

"Tomorrow?" Mother sounded confused.

"All I want to tell you is that Mass will be at 5:00 p.m. We want you to be surprised. Trust your daughters. Will you do that?"

"All right, Millie, I'll do as you say. I'll talk to your father, and we'll both be dressed and ready when you stop for us tomorrow afternoon."

As I told my sisters later, "We wanted to surprise them but now they know. At least we won't have a lot of explaining to do tomorrow."

We brought my parents to Mass at St. Casimir's the next evening, where Father Balczur, who was my father's friend, presided over a procession, and my parents renewed their vows. The priest decorated the church with a gold altar cloth, and he wore a gold *stula*.

When we walked into the Polish Veteran's Hall, I heard a gasp. I turned around and saw Mother standing with her mouth open as she looked at the tables set for 150 guests. "How can you fill all these chairs? We don't have that many friends. Where are you getting all those people?"

As the guests arrived and went through the receiving line, Mother learned they did indeed have enough friends to fill the room. She was surprised by the love they received that night.

Early that morning my sisters and I had decorated the hall with Happy 50th Anniversary signs, tablecloths, napkins and centerpiece trees, all trimmed with gold.

My parents and their three daughters and sons-in-law, their four grandchildren, plus my Aunt Appolonia and Uncle Kasper, were seated at a special head table. Before the dinner, my sister, Lottie, asked our guests to sing a traditional Polish poem, "S*to lat sto lat,*" which translated into "A Hundred Years," to honor Stephanie and Walter.

Then I introduced our 150 guests, explaining how all of them had met my parents. Some were friends from the Polish Veterans Post 40 or from the local chapter of the Polish National Alliance. There were family members from Chicago, neighbors, co-workers and church members.

Waitresses served family style chicken, sausage, sauerkraut, mastocioli, peirogi, potatoes and gravy, salad, plus all kinds of vegetables and home-made pastries. A tiered, gold-trimmed wedding cake was our dessert.

After dinner, all four grandchildren participated in a program for their *babcia* and *dziadziu*. My 15-year-old daughter, Chris, recited a three-stanza poem in Polish to honor her grandparents' 50th anniversary. I don't recall what the poem said, but I do remember my mother was very proud when all the guests applauded. Chris presented her grandmother with a dozen long-stemmed red roses.

My father, who hadn't said too much until now, broke down and cried at the table.

When the band played the anniversary waltz, my father bowed and said, "Stephanie, may I have the honor of the first dance?" To the music of the band and the applause of the guests, he whirled my mother around the floor.

Father then danced with each of his daughters, while Mother was partnered with her three sons-in law. Since we are a family of good dancers, we engaged a wonderful band from Chicago who played polkas, waltzes, tangos, foxtrots or any other music the guests wanted.

Everyone was having such a good time that no one wanted to leave. We paid the band and the hall to stay an extra hour, then another hour, and the clock was striking 4:00 a.m. when we walked in the door at our home.

After the 50th anniversary, Walter and Stephanie had 11 more good years together until my mother died at 80; my father lived until the age of 92.

To the band members who didn't know us, we must have seemed like a typical American middle class family, comfortably well-off, without too many problems or trials in our lives.

Not true. Not even close.

50

STEELMAKING

OTHER VOICES: Author

The first step in steelmaking is to change raw iron ore into iron metal. To do this, iron ore, limestone and coke are layered inside a brick-lined blast furnace that is hundreds of feet high, protruding out of the top of the building. These three ingredients are baked at about 3000 degrees when air is blasted into the bottom of the furnace.

Limestone and the impurities from iron ore form slag. At the bottom of the blast furnace pure molten iron settles with the lighter slag on top. The slag is tapped off first; then the glowing iron is poured out of the bottom.

The men who work in the blast furnace area wear long underwear to keep the heat off their bodies, then their regular clothes, and then aluminum coats down to their ankles. They wear hoods to protect their heads. All day long, these men are working drenched in sweat.

In the next step of steelmaking, the metal is transported to a furnace, most likely to a basic oxygen furnace. A mixture of the molten iron and a small amount of carbon is refined into steel, which is then mixed with various alloys to get the exact steel product of each individual order. Tungsten will be added for heat resistance or molybdenum for corrosion. Manganese gives extra toughness; chromium will make the steel more rust resistant.

Most steel is made in basic oxygen furnaces, huge steel containers lined with heat resistant material. These furnaces can be tilted and turned to add the molten iron, limestone and other alloys. The final product is hot liquid steel, which is solidified and molded into ingots, metal blocks as big as eight feet long and three feet wide, and weighing as much as 300 tons.

Then the glowing hot ingots are rolled or squeezed into beams, bars or slabs at finishing mills. They can be fashioned into railroad rails, I-beams or coils for automobile manufacturing. The largest coil can be 70 or more inches wide and can weigh up to 25 tons.

A hot strip rolling mill can be as long as a mile and a half. The hot slab of steel passes through many sets of rollers that resemble the wringers of an old-fashioned washing machine. The slab will go through the first roller as slowly as a 90-year-old man walks. As the slab moves faster, it gets thinner and longer. By the last roller, the ribbon of steel sheet is paper thin and is moving as fast as an airplane. At the end it smashes into a down coiler which rolls the steel into coils.

In the 1930's there were no continuous rolling mills at Inland Steel. At that time many of the mills were called shape mills. The steel would have to make a U-turn when it reached the end of the building. It had to be turned back the same way from which it came. There was a man whose job was to grab the red hot bar with a set of tongs and feed it to the next set of rollers. If something went wrong, he got his leg burned. That job was so hot that even in the 1930's the men would work only 20 minutes and be off for 20 minutes and on and off all day long. This job required strength.

Steelmaking hasn't changed much for a hundred years because the innovations don't come about that often. One improvement is that safety is more important. In the 1930's a worker would be hurt or killed almost every day.

Steel mill jobs during the depression paid well, and there were always people who thought they could beat the odds.

*   *   *   *   *   *   *   *

Even before steelmaking can begin, the raw materials must be prepared. One of the raw materials used to make steel is coal, which must be changed into coke in a coke plant. The coal is dumped into brick-lined ovens and baked at 3000 degrees.

The first thing that comes off the coal is coal tar. Many by-products are taken from black coal tar— for example: light oils like benzene.

What is left of the coal is called coke. It is pure carbon that looks like coral; it is light and porous.

In 1973, Stephan Rytel was working as a mechanic in Inland Steel Company's coke plant #2. Prior to the creation of OSHA (Occupational Safety and Health Administration), the coke ovens were very smoky from the burning coal, and there was no way for workers to avoid inhaling this smoke. This was the worst place to work in a steel mill because of the tremendous heat and the carcinogenic smoke.

Before 1975, the burning coal and smoke of a coke oven could be smelled a mile away. Everything and everyone in a coke mill would be covered with coal soot mixed with the grease spilled from lubricating the machinery. Even the workers' cars outside would get coated with coal residue. One of the perks for managers was keeping their cars in a garage at work. An employee of the steel plant washed those automobiles.

There were workers whose job it was to clean and degrease the mills because oil could contribute to fires. This was a job that was never finished because there were always new oil spills.

If a man stood off to the side in a coke mill and the smoke was going up, that would not be too uncomfortable for him. However, there is a lot of machinery atop the ovens and the mechanics repairing this high equipment spend a lot of time on the walkways 200 feet in the air. These men would wear shoes with wooden soles two inches thick to insulate their feet from the heat. It's a terribly hot environment; there is no way to be comfortable on that job.

The mechanics don't need great strength—only the strength of a normal man. If something heavy needs to be lifted, machines or cranes do the lifting. Mechanics do need to have mechanical ability.

At Inland Steel in 1973 an apprentice program helped workers acquire knowledge of all the units. The experienced mechanics usually knew how to solve a problem because it had happened before. There were also foremen and engineers to help. If a gear got stripped, the mechanic took out the bad gearbox and put in the spare one. Then they brought the worn gearbox to another location and rebuilt it at their convenience or sent it out to a contractor. Some of the machinery in a coke plant was so large that it needed to be fixed in place, and quickly. In a mill, downtime needed to be minimized.

For working in this dangerous environment with the heat, the smoke and the grease, Stephan Rytel and the other mechanics in a coke mill earned their large paychecks.

After 1975, the tops of the modern coke ovens were sealed much better than they had been previously. The covers on the ovens were opened only to load more coal from the top, and then they were sealed with tar.

Even when coke was not being made, a coke oven was kept hot at all times to prevent the brick lining from shrinking and cracking.

51

THE TELEPHONE CALL

My husband started at Inland Steel as a pipe fitter, but after a few years he was promoted to mechanic in coke plant #2. If anything mechanical broke down at his plant, it was the mechanic's job to fix it. Sometimes Stephan got a call at 2:00 in the morning, and maybe he went in to work for two hours and the bosses punched in four hours for him, but he was required to go.

He went to work smiling like he was going to a wedding—he loved his job that much. He explained to me, "It's never boring because there is always something new to figure out how to fix."

Often two mechanics worked together on a problem. He loved the challenge of finding a solution to any breakdown.

The machinery at work needed to be lubricated every day, and Stephan was constantly working with that greasy equipment. He wore gloves, but sometimes the work was too delicate, and he took them off. His hands were always getting dirty, and he scrubbed them at work with a special soap. We also kept that soap in our basement where he washed his hands again. He was conscientious about keeping his nails clean.

Occasionally he worked 200 feet in the air above a hot oven, wearing an insulated suit to protect himself from the intense heat. He kept extra clothes in his locker so he could change, sometimes two or three times a day.

On about March 1, 1973, Stephan again talked to me about my job. "Millie, I don't like to see you working so hard. I would like it very much if you would quit."

"I like to work," was my answer.

"I know you do. Do you remember when you asked me not to rehab houses because you wanted me to be home with the family? Now I want you at home with me," Stephan said.

"But we can use the extra money for our daughters' college fund," I said.

Stephan gave the perfect answer. "We don't need the extra money. Do you remember when I told you I made a suggestion to improve safety at the mill? Well, they announced today—my idea was awarded $6000, which will be in my paycheck next month. We could save that money in an interest account and use it for the girls' education. Would that please you?" He won me over with that news. "OK," I agreed. "I'll quit my job after Chris and Liz are out of school for the summer."

Stephan smiled and nodded in agreement.

I had been working at the clinic for four years.

On March 8, 1973, Stephen waited up for me to come home from work at 2:00 a.m. That was unusual, because he had to be at work early that next morning. He said, "I miss you. I just know I wanted to see you before I went to bed."

That next morning I fixed his sandwich, and he kissed me goodbye and went to work as usual. I went to the beauty parlor to get my hair done, and there I received the call to go to St. Catherine's Hospital immediately.

52

INLAND FIRE
INJURES 6

Hammond Time
March 8, 1973

Front Page

Inland Fire Injures 6

EAST CHICAGO—Six men were burned today in a fire at Inland Steel Company's Plant No. 2 coke plant.

Two East Chicago fire department engine companies, a ladder truck and two rescue units were called at 9:33 a.m. to fight the blaze. The department left at 10:15 a.m.

Coke oven gas exploded as a gas line was being purged in the north end of the No. 6 coke oven battery basement causing the fire, Inland spokesmen said. Property damage was slight.

The men were taken to St. Catherine Hospital. A hospital spokesman said the burns are bad enough that hospitalization will probably be required.

The injured were identified as:

John Duffy, Floyd Dick, Steve Rytel, Charles Rankin, Richard Snearly and Waver Watson.

53

PURGING THE GAS LINES

OTHER VOICES: Author

All the by-products, like the gases and the smoke, that come off the coal as it is being baked in the coke oven—these by-products have to be routed somewhere. They come out into big pipes, and then they go to precipitators or collectors. If the pipe rusts through after a few years, there will be a hole in that gas pipe, and it will have to be repaired by welding.

The hole can't be isolated and immediately welded because there will still be some residual gases in the pipe, and that would be like setting off a bomb. Purging means to drive out all those gases that are left in the pipe. This can be done with air or with nitrogen. Then tests are taken to make sure the gases are out and there isn't an explosive atmosphere. Only then can workers start working on the pipe.

It's possible that after a line was purged on March 8, 1973, gases were accidentally routed to this line as it was being welded.

In more recent times, the people who purge the line have lock-out equipment secured by a key to keep the lines from being used until the repairs are completed.

Or what may have happened on March 8, 1973, is that all the gases didn't get driven out of the pipe. If a complete purge wasn't effected and if gas was present in the pipe when welding began, there would be an explosion. There could be a fire, depending on where it blew up and what kind of combustible was close to the explosion when it blew.

A burn would feel just as bad if it came from the flash of an explosion or from a fire.

54

KEEPING WATCH AT THE HOSPITAL

While Stephan was at work that next day, March 8, 1973, there was an explosion. Stephan and Charles Rankin, his boss, were not there at the time, but they went to see what they could do to help. There was another explosion behind them, and the two men were caught between the two fires.

At the hospital I wasn't allowed to go in to see him because he was isolated to keep germs away from him. He had burns on 60 per cent of his body. Stephan's boss, who was like a brother to him, died one week later.

I kept watch at Stephan's hospital room every day, along with shifts of his friends. In the morning I took the kids to school and then I went to the hospital and stayed there until 11:00 or 12:00 at night.

Since Stephan was isolated, the only way I could communicate with him was through the intercom at the nurses' station. He wasn't able to speak every day, but when he did talk he was concerned about our daughters, and he wanted to know all about them and how they were doing. Nearly every day I read loving letters to him from our Chris and Liz.

They might write: *We miss you, Daddy. We love you. Please get better and come home soon. Love, Chris and Liz*

"Go home and watch the children," he would tell me. He would add, "Don't worry about me. Take care of our daughters."

One thing he was concerned about was Inland Steel, because he didn't trust his company. He insisted, "Do not sign any papers they give you."

I wasn't sure what he meant by that, but I promised, "OK, Stephan, I will do as you say." I intended to respect his wishes, but I also knew that my promise would calm him.

It wasn't often that I could talk to him. Most of the time I sat in a chair outside his room looking through the peephole in the door.

Then one Wednesday evening they let me in to see him, and I found him sitting up in a chair, swathed in bandages. His hands and face, and everything else I could see, were burned. He was semi-conscious and I tried to give him water, which he couldn't drink. I told him, "I love you."

He said, "I love you, too." Then all of a sudden he got weak and fainted, so I was asked to leave the room.

At this point I was so exhausted that his friends at the hospital convinced me to go home and get some rest. I drove to our house by myself, and when I got there I saw the kids were sleeping, so I didn't want to make any noise. I couldn't sleep, but finally I nodded off. At 5:00 that Thursday morning, March 22, 1973, the phone rang. Of course the girls woke up, and they were upset. The caller said, "Mrs. Rytel, I'm sorry. Your husband has passed away. We need you to come to the hospital right away to accept the body."

I told the children, "Daddy died," and I collapsed. When I came to, I said to my daughters, "I will kill everybody in my path if I try to drive to the hospital myself."

Chris went to a neighbor, Stephan's cousin, who lived next door to us. He came, gave us a ride to the hospital to accept the body and helped us to decide on a mortuary.

I wasn't prepared for Stephan's death, and somehow I was in denial about what was happening. I realize now that the hospital people wouldn't suddenly have let me in his room to see him unless he was near death and unless the germs wouldn't matter anymore.

55

MILL BURNS KILL MAN

Hammond Time
March 23, 1973
Front Page

Mill Burns Kill Man

EAST CHICAGO—A Hammond man died today of injuries suffered in a March 8 fire at Inland Steel Company's Plant No. 2 Coke plant.

He was Steven Rytel, 49, 555 Schneider Avenue.

Coke oven gas exploded as a gas line was being purged.

Charles Rankin, 61, of 555 No. Arbogast, Griffith, died a week ago from injuries suffered in the fire.

Four other men were injured.

(Obituary, Page 2)

CALUMET REGION OBITUARIES

RYTEL
   Stephan Rytel, age 49, of 555 Schneider Ave., Hammond, Ind., passed away Thursday, March 22, 1973, at St. Catherine's Hospital. Survivors: wife, Millie (nee Zygmunt); two daughters, Christine and Elizabeth at home; parents, Frank and Sophie Rytel in Poland; parents-in-law, Wladyslaw and Stephania Zygmunt of Hammond; two sisters-in-law, Mrs. Lucille (Karol) Krupa of Hammond and Mrs. Lottie (John) Koziel of Placentia, Calif.; several nieces, nephews and cousins.
   Funeral services Saturday March 24, 9:30 a.m. from the Dziadowicz and Anthony Funeral Home, 4404 Cameron Ave., Hammond, 10 a.m. St. Casimir Church, Rev. Anthony Balczur officiating. Burial, Holy Cross Cemetery, Calumet City. Friends may call at the Chapel Friday, 2 to 5 and 7 to 10pm.
   He was a Hammond resident for the past 24 years; an employee of Inland Steel Company; a member of the Polish National Alliance and the Steel Workers Union Local 1010.

56

HEAVY BLACK FOG

Mr. Dziadowicz was a cousin of my brother-in-law, and we chose him for Stephan's funeral director. He told me, "You are in no condition to have a two-day wake because you are too exhausted." On his advice we decided on a one-day viewing.

Stephan was coated with makeup to cover the burns on his face and hands. This meant we were not allowed to give him a kiss—I couldn't even kiss my husband goodbye.

At the time of Stephan's death, there was a cruel law which stated that the banks were required to read the obituaries and immediately freeze any account with the decedent's name on it. Our funeral director knew I would need money to survive. On that Friday morning, the day after Stephan died, Mr. Dziadowicz warned me, "Get a ride to your bank right away and change the names on your accounts from Stephan Rytel and Millie Rytel, to Millie Rytel and Walter Zygmunt. Your children are not old enough to sign." My brother-in-law drove me and my father to the bank.

The people at the bank probably wondered what was going on, but of course I couldn't tell them. It seemed to me that everyone was looking at me as if to ask what I was doing,

When I got home from the bank on that Friday morning, Inland Steel called me, "Come in and pay for health insurance for yourself and your daughters if you want to keep that coverage."

I didn't want another errand on the day of the wake, but I knew our insurance was needed for my family. Ironically, later I realized I also had health insurance at the clinic where I worked, but I couldn't think my way out of the heavy black fog surrounding me.

As a friend of my father's, Father Balczur often went to my parent's home to spend time talking to Walter. We had the funeral at St. Casimir's rather than at my new parish.

We bought the most expensive casket they had-- $3000. I said, "Stephan deserves the best because he has earned it." Now I realize he would have wanted his children and me to be kept financially secure with what money we had. He would have wanted our savings to go towards our childrens' education. Again, the black fog interfered with my thinking.

The luncheon after the funeral was at St. Casimir's. Father Balczur refused to charge me for the use of the church hall. "I have to pay you something," I told him, and I finally gave him a check for $25.

My stunned, grief-stricken mother and father called my sister Lottie, and thank goodness she flew to Indiana from California to be with me. Although she was also upset, she was able to stand up at the funeral luncheon and say, "Thank you, everyone, for coming to the funeral, for the food you brought, and especially for your kind words of sympathy.

Because there were so many relatives, and my family knew so many people from our churches, neighborhoods and jobs, Stephan's funeral was attended by more people than any previous funeral that mortuary had ever handled.

I wasn't able to make the arrangements for my husband's wake and funeral luncheon, and others did that job for me. The tradition in 1973 at most Polish funeral luncheons was to serve cocktails, and this luncheon got out of hand with the drinking. Some people drank too much liquor and they needed to be helped out. One man passed out in the hallway, which made my grief even sadder.

With the cost of the wake and the funeral, the bill came to $10,000 in 1973 dollars—I almost fainted when I saw that amount. I was grieving, and I was not making good decisions.

Inland Steel sent a beautiful, tall, showy floral arrangement with birds of paradise and other tropical flowers. I took out my frustrations with Stephan's company by telling the funeral director, "I want that arrangement thrown out right after the funeral."

Stephan's company also gave me a beautiful white Bible in a cedar case. I was numb in my black grief, and I misread the sympathy card that came with it. I didn't realize the truth until 2005, when my author asked me to check the color of the Bible. That book was from the Steelworkers Union #1010. After 32 years, I am now finally able to treasure that inspiring gift.

After Stephan's death, so many people wanted to help, and their kindnesses softened my grief a little. Food from friends, relatives and neighbors filled the refrigerator and the freezer, as well as the kitchen counters and tables. Casseroles, salads, desserts, side dishes, and stews were everywhere. There were so many caring people.

The food we couldn't eat or freeze, I gave to my co-workers at the clinic. "How much can three of us use?" I asked my daughters. I couldn't even swallow a drop of water at that time, much less eat anything.

There were also many good people who sent cards and expressed their sympathy with caring words. But there was one bitter man who had always been jealous of our happy marriage. He said, "Stephan deserved to die." I was so hurt by his meanness that I shed tears every time I thought about him.

My Aunt Appolonia and Uncle Kasper planned their 50th wedding anniversary celebration for just one month after my husband died. This was my favorite Aunt Appolonia who sponsored us when we came to America. She loaned us the money to get here and she invited us to live in her house. She organized cousins and uncles to help. She found jobs for us and picked out our first apartment. She introduced us to most of our acquaintances, and thanks to her we had instant friends when we arrived.

I was scheduled to be the Mistress of Ceremonies at her 50th anniversary party. I bought a new dress for the occasion, and my husband was helping me plan what I was going to say.

My grief was so heavy that a week or two before her party, I told her, "I just can't honor my commitment to preside at your party. I'm not an actress, and I know my emotions will show through and ruin your celebration."

Unfortunately for both of us, she didn't understand. This caused a rift between us that was not healed for a year and a half.

I sat in the back row of the church for Kasper and Appolonia's anniversary mass, and I cried through the whole ceremony. I did everyone a favor by not attending the party later. I told my daughters, "You can go if you wish," but they also chose not to be there. In my place as Master of Ceremonies, my aunt and uncle engaged the secretary of the local chapter of the Polish National Alliance. Although he did a wonderful job, my aunt somehow couldn't understand I was hurting so much that I didn't have the courage to stand up and talk.

Aunt Appolonia thought I betrayed her and she stopped talking to me. She didn't invite me to parties in her home, although my sister was asked. My mother was hurt by our rift and tried, without success, to smooth things over.

I'll tell you the truth. I may not have gone to any parties if I was invited. Although I was very lonely, I pushed people away even while I needed them. Sometimes I locked myself in my bedroom when my parents came on the bus to see me. I felt broken.

My parents were also traumatized by Stephan's death. They loved him like the son they never had. I could have used my father's advice with business decisions, but perhaps because he wasn't raised in this country and wasn't proficient in English, I was on my own for a lot of problems.

Inland Steel Company's insurance paid for his hospital bills. However, according to the terms of the present contract, I was entitled to no pension because Stephan was a year short of being vested in their retirement fund, even though he had worked for his company for 24 years.

In March of 1973 the Steel Worker's Union Local 1010 and Inland Steel signed a new contract that stated, "If a worker dies on the job, his widow will get half of his pension." The steelworkers approved this new agreement, which was to go into effect on April 1, 1973. Unfortunately for his family, Stephan died on March 22, 1973, just nine days before.

We did receive Social Security for my daughters for as long as they were in school. We also received $240 monthly in Workman's Compensation until both children reached the age of 18.

Ironically, because Stephan was killed on the job, and because we were receiving Workman's Compensation, we were only entitled to half of his life insurance, a total of $13,000. Had he died of a heart attack at home, we would have received the whole $26,000.

The funeral's $10,000 bill was due to be paid, and I had not yet received the $6000 check from Inland Steel for Stephan's safety suggestion. I was so thankful I could count on that money coming in.

"Inland Steel Employee Relations," the voice answered the phone when I called.

"This is Millie Rytel, Stephan's widow. I called to ask when you'll be sending the $6000 check for his safety suggestion."

"Will you hold for a minute please?" the voice asked.

"Mrs Rytel," a second person said, "we will not be sending that $6000 check, because the rules state that a suggestion award winner must be an employee of Inland Steel at the time of the payment. Mr.Rytel is no longer employed by our company. I'm sorry.

"Sorry! Sorry?" I screamed. "That's my money. If you don't give it to me, you'll be hearing from my lawyers. Then YOU will be sorry."

Stephan's award-winning idea was a suggestion to improve safety. I asked my father a question that was haunting my mind, "Would Stephan's safety plan, had it been implemented, have saved his life?" Father couldn't tell me, and I'll never know the answer to that mystery.

We could see that I wouldn't be getting much money from Stephan's company. I was planning to quit my job, but of course, now I couldn't. I needed to work. Everyone assumed that I would get a large settlement from Inland Steel.

I took the train into Chicago all by myself to hire a law firm to represent me and my daughters. I didn't want them to miss out on college because we couldn't afford to pay for it. Also, I had no pension to live on when I got older.

We fought Inland Steel for seven years, but our lawyers finally told me it was no use. For some reason I don't understand, Indiana law protected the employer instead of the employee if that worker was killed on the job. "If the company was in any other state, you would be financially secure with

several million dollars or more," my lawyers told
me.

57

THE BULLY

About this time, my daughter in elementary
school became very unhappy, and she suffered from
fainting spells. When we went to the doctor, he
gave her many tests like an electroencephalogram,
but he couldn't find anything wrong with her. He
suggested, "Maybe something is bothering her."

When I asked her if she had a problem, she kept
everything inside and wouldn't talk to me. "I have
no problems," was all she would say.

Meanwhile, her teacher wrote on her report
card, "She is sullen, disruptive and uncooperative in
school."

I decided I would talk to the other children to
see what I could find out. So one by one, I quietly
asked the kids, "What is my daughter doing in
school that is so disruptive?"

They all said the same thing. "She isn't doing
anything wrong. She is being pushed around at
school by a mean bully. She is being wrongly
blamed for any noises or talking in the classroom."

The bully took her lunch money, saying,
"You're supposed to eat breakfast. If you ate
breakfast, you wouldn't need to eat lunch."

As a teenager, I was made to suffer hunger and thirst. We survived abuse and indignity. We were worked like animals. I had been to hell and back. I swore, "With God as my witness, no daughter of mine is going to be unhappy. In this free country, my child is not going to be bullied by anyone as I had been."

The next afternoon after school, I confronted the bully in my daughter's classroom. I shouted, "I found out about all the mean things you're doing. I know you're picking on my daughter, and you're going to stop. You will treat her like you treat all the other kids. If your bullying doesn't stop, I'll be back to yell at you every day. Is that clear?"

I have a loud voice, and I made such a commotion that the principal came to see what all the ruckus was about. I told her, "Get out. This is between the two of us."

After I set the matter straight and the school administration found out what was going on, they supported me. My daughter recovered, and her fainting spells stopped.

When I asked her why she wouldn't tell me what was wrong, she replied, "You have so many problems right now—I didn't want to add to your worries."

And why, you ask, didn't the teacher realize what was going on and stop the bully?

Because the teacher was—The Bully.

58

MY LIFE GOES ON

For the sake of my daughters, I needed to go on with my life. I had to put one foot in front of the other. I planned to quit my job at the end of the school year, but now I needed to work to support my family. Even though I enjoyed working, now it felt like a big responsibility to me.

The manager of the clinic was very understanding when I needed time off from work with sick children or a business problem. He told me, "I have met your husband, and I respected him." Those words helped me. Also, there was a European-born doctor who would listen when I needed to talk.

There were times when the blackness in my heart was so heavy that I needed to get out of the house that Stephan built. Thank goodness I could drive. Sometimes I went to Woodmar Shopping Center and just walked around, which somehow made me feel a little less sad. I had saved all the cards from flowers and presents that Stephan gave me, and I often looked at them when I felt especially lonely.

I was having a hard time with the family's paper work. I never did any of our check writing or bookkeeping because Stephan took care of everything. I didn't even know what bills we were paying. My father helped a lot, but he was limited by his lack of English. My oldest daughter, Chris, was 16 years old and a junior in high school, and she took over half of her father's jobs—the financial paperwork and bookkeeping. For tax purposes, we needed to keep track of the expenses for our two duplexes.

After Stephan died, I wrote to his parents every week. They lived in a very old house that was still located in Poland. I told about how the kids were doing. I expressed myself about my husband and how much I missed him. When his mother wrote back, she also poured out her grief to me. If it's possible, she was even more torn up by Stephan's death than I was, and she died of a broken heart five years after she lost her son.

When Stephan's mother passed away, I continued to write to his father, and I never sent just the letter. I would always send a little money, like $10, which was a big amount for me at that time. Although his eyes were getting bad, he scribbled his thanks and said, "Please keep writing to me." He was so grateful.

The other Polish cousins told me, "Stephan's father is being neglected."

I was occupied with the kids, the house, and I also took care of the duplexes. Sometimes I worked at the clinic six days a week, and even though I was very busy, it was important to me to sit down and write to my father-in-law every week. Showing honor to Stephan's dad was my way of expressing my love to my husband.

The letter and the money gave him better treatment with his cousins in Poland who inherited his farm on the condition they take care of him until he died. It gave him a lift and it got him some respect. He waited for those letters, even though he would have to ask someone to read them to him.

Stephan's father lived to the age of 92. I told my daughters, "I think my husband would also have lived a long life if he hadn't been hurt on his job. We could have enjoyed a long happy marriage." But the reality was that my husband was in Heaven, while I was here on Earth with problems to solve.

Stephan's cousin helped me with mechanical or electrical emergencies around the house. I didn't want there to be any misunderstandings about money with anyone, so I offered to pay for this help. Sometimes he accepted money, but most of the time he didn't.

And I learned. Once when the light in the oven burned out, I was unscrewing the bulb and it broke. I tried to get the glass shards out of the socket and got knocked to the floor on my keister. After that shock, I learned to turn off the electricity before doing anything electrical.

I got an education in other ways as well. There was an older guy who lived near me who kept bringing me vegetables, apples or other things. It turned out he wanted us to be friends—you know, really friendly friends. He wanted sex.

"This is the last time you will ever set foot inside my home, the house that Stephan built," I told him. "You have a wife. You have kids. Go home to them."

I was 47 years old, and he was 20 years older and married. I wasn't pretty, and I wasn't rich. I was vulnerable, but I wasn't stupid. His advances were cruel because I needed friends at this time. In my sensitive state, I often couldn't think, but this time I knew exactly what to say.

And I made some mistakes. When my 16-year-old daughter was invited to the prom, I wouldn't let her go because we were in mourning. She was having a difficult enough time as it was. I realized later that not being able to do her normal teenage activities just made her adjustment even harder.

Some months after Stephan died, Inland Steel sent me $3000, half of the $6000 suggestion award money. "I'm giving up. I'm cashing the check and taking this money," I told my father.

"Yes, Millie, having an end to thinking about that $6000 will help you heal," Father agreed.

When Kasper, Appolonia's husband, got sick about 18 months after Stephan's death, I heard from my family that he wasn't doing well at all. I'd always liked Uncle Kasper and he liked me. He was quiet, but he was a very good man who would always give his heart to others. He genuinely enjoyed people, and I knew I must visit him. He was so happy to see me that he welcomed me with a big hug.

My aunt said, "Thank you for coming to see my husband," and just like that we were now friends again. I think we were both relieved that our long rift was healed. Our reconciliation took a big load off the shoulders of my parents.

For a long time I didn't go anywhere socially. Then, two years after Stephan's death, there was an

Easter party and my parents, sister and brother-in-law were going. "Millie, why don't you come with us?" my mother asked. "It will be a nice change for you."

After listening to my parents and sister talk about the party, I decided, "OK, I'll go, but I'm driving by myself so I can escape when I want."

At the party, this man named Ed came over and asked me to dance. I started to say, "No, thank you."

Everyone else said, "Yes, she'd love to," and many hands pushed me onto the floor. I didn't think I was ready, but we danced and several days later he started calling me. He got me out of the house and took me to movies, dances and restaurants. He was very generous to me and my children—I have to be grateful to him for that. I saw him for about ten years until he died.

About this time, I chaperoned Liz' high school class on a cruise. I liked it so much that I tried to organize my whole family to go on a cruise with me.

My father said, "Take your mother, have a good time, but don't ask me."

"Don't ask me either," added my mother.

Lottie and Lucille decided, "No, thank you."

My parents and sisters were seasick on the ocean and wanted nothing to do with water, and there could be no cruise.

I plunged into my work at the clinic and at home. I was kept busy cleaning up after our tenants at our duplexes. There were always floors to scrub, things to fix, and painters to hire. One renter stored tires in the living room. Some owned pets that ruined the wooden floors. Once I worked to get a unit all painted and repaired, and two days later the renters had already trashed it.

Sometimes I would agree to meet potential renters at a certain time. I would drive all the way to the units in Schererville, taking time off from work, and they wouldn't show up. "This constant hassle over managing these properties is getting to me. I can't take it anymore," I told my father. I sold the duplexes 11 years after Stephan died. I just wanted to be rid of the responsibility of taking care of them.

My father came to help at my house, especially with the outdoor jobs. Sometimes in the morning I'd be out buying groceries and when I came home, he was there. The lawn mower was running and the hedge clippers were out, ready to trim the bushes. He said, "I came. I've got nothing else to do. I want to help you with your yard work." Bless my father.

His hobby was trimming the bushes for his entire neighborhood. I protested, "You shouldn't have to cut all those branches."

His answer was, "I love to work outside."

Other times when I asked for help, I picked him up at his house, because neither my father nor my mother learned to drive. When my father came to help me, he often rode one bus and transferred in downtown Hammond to another line. Or he got someone to drop him off. My mother came by bus to stay with my daughters when I needed to get away by myself. She told me, "I wanted to help clean your house, but it is already spotless."

My parents didn't want to learn to drive because of the expense. "Besides, I'm too old to learn," Father said.

Wherever they wanted to go, my sister or I would give them rides. Mother loved to walk to church unless the weather was bad. When friends called to offer a ride, Father always found a way to repay them in some other way.

Photo #9 - Courtesy of Thomas J. Hoolehan

Walter and Millie

My father was there for us in 1988 to walk my daughter, Liz, down the aisle. He was not feeling well, but he didn't tell anyone. He said, "I am honored to do the job that Stephan can't. I'm proud to be part of Liz' wedding."

He was too sick to travel to California to give my Chris away when she was married in 1991. I flew to the west coast to attend my daughter's wedding.

And slowly the happy and fun times started pushing away the black fog.

59

WALTER AND STEPHANIE

My father, Walter Zygmunt, was an active, outgoing person who liked to entertain family groups with his stories and jokes. He knew how to phrase his words to bring out the punch line.

He was very fluent in Polish and Russian. He had a chance to use his language skills when his company hired Lithuanians, and he would talk to them in Russian. His Russian was much better than his broken English.

As he made friends with the Lithuanian men, Walter listened as his co-workers began to share information about their backgrounds. My father was amazed to find that some of them had replaced us as slaves in *Nizhnya Striga,* the same Siberian labor camp where we were kept. Father didn't tell us how or when these people were released, because these experiences were too painful to repeat.

Walter was active in the Polish National Alliance, becoming president of Council 49. He was an officer in the Polish Veterans Association, Post 40. If these organizations had any activity going on, he was always there to help. When they sponsored a carnival, he took the bus straight from work to help set up, sometimes not getting home until 11:00 or 12:00 at night.

Father often stopped at Vogel's Restaurant, where my mother worked, to have dinner. She was the dishwasher, and her job included lifting heavy stacks of dishes into the washer and onto shelves. When he realized how hard her job was, he decided, "You're staying home. You're not working any longer."

She had worked for about eight years in this country, and she was happy to quit.

After he arrived in the United States, Father was very careful to stay slim and fit. He was very vain about his looks, often cutting down on food if he noticed any sign of a paunchy stomach. He always dressed in a shirt and tie when he went to church or to parties, and his young grandchildren loved to look at their reflection in his shiny shoes.

Father was a heavy smoker during the war. After he had lived in America for six years, he got very sick with stomach ulcers. His doctor decreed, "Quit smoking."

He quit cold turkey. My mother made sure he stayed on the doctor's strict diet, and in two years, he regained his health. As sick as he was, he never stopped working.

At the age of 67, Walter was vested into General American's retirement fund, and he retired.

His pension was $100 per month, plus his and Stephanie's Social Security. As a World War II veteran, he also received a small pension from England. My parents lived frugally, so their income allowed them to make several trips to Poland and to Lottie's house in California.

Lottie and my parents went to see the Queen Mary when it was docked in Los Angeles. The ship was completely refitted from when they were onboard in 1950.

Both of my parents' schooling stopped at the sixth grade, but they were well educated because they liked to read. My mother wanted to better herself, and there was not one Polish book in the whole Chicago-Hammond area that my father hadn't read. After retirement he always held a book in his hands when he wasn't working outside in the garden. Walter Zygmunt, with perfect Polish grammar and pronunciation, was chosen to read Books for People on tapes in that language.

Walter and Stephanie were a lot alike, and they kept harmony in their house. Sometimes they would have a fight and not talk to each other for a day or two, but that was unusual. They were both strong-willed, but Father was more stubborn, like me. Mother usually gave in and made peace.

One time she did put her foot down. For many years, Walter cherished a dream. "I want to buy a small farm in America when I retire."

My mother said, "Go ahead, honey, I'll give you my blessing, but I'm staying right here where I am."

And Stephanie stayed in her house until she passed away in 1983 at the age of 80.

Because of his well-groomed appearance and because he was always courtly to the ladies, more than one woman was interested in the new widower. One widow of about my age was determined to catch him. My father saw through her plans, which he did not share, and he simply told her, "Go away," and she went.

As he reached his late eighties, Walter was nearly blind with macular degeneration. Some people told me, "You should put your father in a retirement home." I would never have gotten over the guilt if I forced him to move. Besides, he was nearly self-sufficient in his home. He rose an hour early on Sundays and shaved over and over again until he could feel that his face was smooth.

I helped him by cleaning his house and by taking him shopping.

My father carried in his heart one wish that was never fulfilled. He often said, "Before I die, I want to go back to Russia and find Teresa's grave."

Of course, he knew in his mind this wasn't possible because the burial site was marked only with a wooden cross with her name on it, which would be long gone after nearly 50 years.

When Father died in 1993 at the age of 92, he had lived in America for 40 years. God granted him a lot more than he prayed for as a slave in Siberia. "Please God, for just one day before I die, let me have enough bread to eat so that I'm not hungry."

60

POLISH CULTURE

I have been a member of the Polish National Alliance for 55 years. This organization encourages Polish customs and traditions, but it is fiercely loyal to the United States.

They have a fraternal life insurance company. The profits from this company are used for college scholarships, programs and sports for the Polish-American youth. Orphanages, schools and hospitals

Photo #10

Millie at PNA convention

in Poland also receive some support from the Polish National Alliance. They have two banks that operate like credit unions, because they pay a higher rate of return for savers, but they give a lower interest rate for borrowers. There is a Polish language radio station.

The Polish National Alliance is my favorite organization. They have conventions every four

Photo #11

Millie with award

years, and I have gone to these meetings nine times. I would do anything for the members of that organization, because I love those people. They accepted me immediately as an equal when we first came to this country. Some of them went through the same hard times in the 1940s that we did.

When people are ill, I visit hospitals and send cards. There are too many visits and too many cards now at this time of my life.

In the Polish National Alliance, I have been president of Council 49 for 35 years, and my father was president before me. In Lodge 3095, which I helped organize, I've been the recording secretary for 46 years.

I met Mayor McDermott, Sr. of Hammond, because the Polish National Alliance and the Polish Veterans always invited the mayor to our Christmas parties. He sat at the head table, sometimes next to me. He did not belong to the same political party as I did, but he suggested I apply to be an election judge. It was my privilege to work at elections for the next six or seven years, even though I was not born in the United States. Along with the other judges, I made sure the election was fair.

Voting is the most important thing a citizen can do. It is a privilege, because you can express yourself. You have the freedom to vote for whomever you want although you may not get your choice because other people don't agree with you. Nobody can tell you what to do. In Communist countries there was just one candidate who thought he was God. Every Russian was forced to vote anyway. If he didn't, he was punished. The Soviet regime even decreed where everyone was forced to shop.

In the United States, we can do anything we want, as long as we are not hurting someone else. This country is what freedom is all about. I have enjoyed so many opportunities here.

Once when Senator Ted Kennedy came to the Gary Airport, I was asked by the mayor to sit on the dais as a representative of the Polish people.

For 40 years I have been a delegate to the Polish American Congress, which is an "umbrella" organization encompassing all the Polish unions.

For 36 years I have been a member of the Ladies Auxiliary Post 40 of the Polish Veterans.

In 2006, along with 22 others from Post 40, I

Photo #12

Millie, flag bearer - 2000

was privileged to be a delegate to their convention in Boston. There were two days of business sessions, and on Saturday night we enjoyed a dinner-dance.

One of the men, who was 18 inches taller than my five feet, came over and kidded me, "I would ask you to dance, but somehow I don't think we would fit too well."

We both laughed, "Look at my left arm straight up in the air. This is where my hand would have to be on your shoulder." I accepted another invitation to dance with a short man.

Thinking it over later, I believe Mr. Tall and I could have figured out another position for my arm.

The dance floor was packed, which shows that old Polish people still know how to have a good time. However, the main reason I enjoyed this convention was because I was with people who are smarter than I am.

Photo #13

Millie at reunion - 1964

Another fun activity has been the many reunions
of the Polish refugees who were in Africa. I've
gone to three of them. The first one in Munster,
Indiana, at the Carmelite Fathers Sanctuary, had
approximately 2000 attendees of all ages. The kind
American priest who was in Africa with us also
came to that reunion. We were all dressed in new
clothes, showing off that America was good to us. It
is so wonderful to have elegant clean clothes, a
pleasure that was denied us for such a long time.

Some refugees came from Australia, where they
used the skills they learned in Poland to become
very successful farmers. They said to us, "Australia
gave us free land and the start-up resources we
needed, as well as the freedom to work as we
wished." Because the Polish refugees were
ambitious, some of them became wealthy.

My next reunion, in Posen, Canada, was not
attended by too many people, although a lot of
Polish refugees were proud to adopt Canada as their
new country.

Our 50th reunion was in Pennsylvania at a
college where we stayed in dorms. People change
after a half century, so everyone wore nametags
with their maiden name, married name and
hometown. My lady friend, who was living with us
in the orphanage at Camp Tengeru, is the national
president of the Ladies Auxiliary of Polish
Veterans, and her husband is the commander for the
Polish Veterans for all of America.

I have done a lot of traveling in the world.
When my youngest daughter was out of high
school, I traveled with Lottie's California group.

We cruised on the Mediterranean Sea, seeing the Holy Land, Paris, Spain and Portugal.

Twice I have been back to Poland. I toured the country on my own in 1978, visiting some of my relatives who were still living. I think that is when I learned that the Communist government turned my parents' immaculate farm into a commune. I never went back to see how our home looked now. I decided, "I was meant to remember our property as it was during my childhood."

Lottie, John and I took a pre-arranged tour of Poland in the 1980's, when we saw Warsaw and Krakow. During our trip to Poland, we made contact with the Bishop of Wroclaw, who was a young priest at our church when we were growing up in Hallerczyn. He came to our hotel with his brother, Stanley, who asked the three of us, "Will you come to my house for a home-cooked dinner tomorrow night?" We remembered Stanley, his wife and their young family when they were our neighbors in the old country. He told us his wife died some years before.

"Thank you. It would be fun to have a meal at your house and to reminisce about old times," we agreed.

Stanley and a lady friend served us a very good dinner, at which he started paying a lot of special romantic attention to me. As a guest in his home, I didn't want to be rude to him, but I wasn't interested. He was about 15 years older than I was, and I could see he was living with the woman. I didn't need any relationship with him.

I wanted to say, "Stanley, you must think I'm stupid. I know you want a meal ticket to come to

America. I have as much responsibility as I can handle taking care of myself and helping my family. I don't need an old man as a dependent." I didn't say those rude words, but I did let him know, "My life is complete as it is. I am not interested."

When the dinner party broke up, Lottie, John and I thanked our host and hostess, and I was able to escape back to our hotel.

The next day's tour took us to a museum to see a special exhibit of beautiful 15th century tapestries, and surprise, Stanley showed up there. My sister was married, so she was safe. Stanley headed straight to me. "Lottie, please save me," I pleaded.

Lottie tried to help by standing between us when she could. Stanley kept moving back to my side, refusing to take "no" for an answer. He was so persistent that I hid out in the ladies' room. "Leave Millie alone. She's not interested in you," Lottie begged, but Stanley wouldn't go home. I came out of the restroom, and I tried to sneak away from the museum, but he was right behind me. This man was desperate to get to the United States, and he had just two days to win me over before we left his city. "Go away. Leave me alone. Go home to your lady friend," I shouted.

We were trying to keep this disagreement quiet from our tourist group, but some of them could understand Polish and knew what was happening. Some of them started chanting in Polish, "She doesn't want you. She doesn't want you." That got through to Stanley, and he gave up and went home. I was now free to enjoy the rest of the tour.

This trip taught me one thing. I want Poland and its citizens to prosper, but now all my loyalty is to the United States.

Photo #14

Lucille, Millie and Lottie

Back home again, I started seeing Al in 1988, after we met at the Hammond Senior Citizens Club. His father was German and his mother was Polish, but he does not speak the Polish language.

I like to travel to California to see Chris and her children. My sister, Lottie, also lives in that state, and I visit her on every trip. We often meet in Las Vegas. I have also been invited to Cousin Mary's house in California.

In Indiana I have watched Liz' three children since they were born. They like it when I cook for them. One family activity I do not enjoy is going with my daughter and grandchildren to the zoo. I saw all of these animals in the wild, and I would

Photo #15

Grandchildren

like to remember them running free in big herds or flying gracefully in flocks.

My six-year-old granddaughter asked questions about husbands and wives. I told her, "When you grow up, you have to be very careful whom you pick for a husband. He has to be kind and loving, because he won't change after the marriage."

Their dog's name is Cookie, and sometimes I take care of him. He is so cute, and he loves to put his paws on my shoulder and kiss me on the face. I tell people, "I don't want to be kissed by a dog," but I like it too.

After I take him for a walk to do his business, I tell him, "Now you have to go to your room." He is so smart. He obeys and gets into his cage. He knows he is not allowed to have the run of the house when his masters are gone. He also knows I always give him a treat, which costs money for me, but he is worth it.

I cannot stop being frugal with money or possessions because my mind takes me back to Russia like it was yesterday. I'll never get over that feeling of hunger. When someone is hungry, he is desperate. He doesn't care what he has to do to get something to eat. He'll do anything, even risk his life. He doesn't stop to consider the consequences.

I have a hard time with leftovers. To keep from throwing dried bread away, I grate it into crumbs to use as a topping on vegetables or in soup. I feel like I'm committing a sin if I throw any food away. When I have to get rid of stale bread or leftovers, I feel guilty because so many people are hungry. I put it in the garbage while I think about something else, like I am hiding my actions from myself.

There are people who own more possessions that I do, but I have never been jealous. I'm satisfied with what I have. Possessions are good, but they're not that important. Most people in America have more money than I do, but that's not what life is about. I enjoy my family and friends, and when I want to socialize, they are there for me.

I am jealous of anyone who has a good marriage. I don't want to break them up; I simply wish I enjoyed a relationship like theirs. It's easy to see when a husband and wife truly care for each other just by the way they hold hands or their eyes meet. I wish I could have that closeness again, but I have a good life with my children and grandchildren. And I'm lucky that I have been an American for more than 50 years.

What would my life have been like if I had chosen to stay in Russia with Latonia?

61

MILLIE IN THE NEIGHBORHOOD

OTHER VOICES: Author

Within minutes after I met Millie in 2000, I was fighting with her.

The freezing February day my husband and I moved into our new paired cottage, the doorbell rang. A coatless Millie was locked out of her house next door when the wind pressure pulled her door shut and locked.

I called the home builder's office. "We'll send someone with a master key, but it might be an hour or so," they said.

Millie announced, "I'll wait outside."

I disagreed, "You will wait in my warm house."

She asserted again that she would wait outside.

I decided, "You will wait inside my house if I have to tie you to a chair."

She waited inside.

Millie's heavy accent told my husband and me that she was from somewhere in Europe. The only thing she would say about her background was, "I came from Poland."

Then one day, after we had known Millie for more than four years, she came to our home and just started talking. Her story poured out of her like the stream over a stony waterfall, tumbling and turning, skipping and twisting. And that is how I came to write her painful history.

Working on this book with Millie was often slow-going, because she kept turning off the tape recorder while she sobbed. I said to my husband, "My God, what harm am I doing to this woman?"

I asked a counselor friend for guidance. She said, "It will lessen Millie's pain if she can talk it out."

This was the first time she had ever talked about her stolen teenage years. I think the counselor was right. I sincerely believe that telling her story has been therapeutic for Millie. She often said, "My daughters don't know . . . . ."

One of her daughters agreed, "Writing her story is good for Mother, and her grandchildren will benefit from knowing what she went through."

Her memory has not dulled much over time. She recalls the traumatic things in her life in great detail.

I didn't know much about Polish history and heritage, and as Millie's story unfolded, I have learned a great respect for the Polish refugee immigrants.

In the 21st century, Millie lives frugally in her immaculately scrubbed and polished house. However, her car is something to behold. It is not allowed to have even one speck of dirt anywhere on it, and it is the shiniest 12-year-old automobile in the state. She takes her car to an auto body shop the minute it develops any rust.

Her daughters are both successful professional women who use the college education Millie insisted they have. Her five grandchildren are a particular joy to her. She has two granddaughters in California. Her other young grandchildren, two boys and a girl, live near her in Indiana. When they were young, she would often baby sit for them, as well as driving them to their activities. She loves helping out with the family dog.

Millie gets up at 5:00 every morning to go to the Hammond Health Club in the Civic Center to exercise for an hour and a half.

Whenever her condo homeowner's association has a workday, Millie is right there to help.

Millie has a gentlemen caller with whom she goes to dances or just out to eat. Al invites her to go with him to Las Vegas, where he gambles and she does not. During his rehabilitation from open heart surgery in 2005, Millie spent four weeks nursing him back to health in her home.

As of this writing, she is still an officer in several of her Polish organizations, for which she also attends national conventions.

Occasionally Millie will complain that she is so tired. "Why are you tired?" her neighbors ask her.

"Well, we danced until 1:00 this morning."

There is no sympathy in the neighborhood for any senior who is tired the next day after dancing until 1:00 a.m.

62

DINNER WITH THE PRESIDENT

In 2006, Mr. Lech Kaczynski, the newly-elected President of Poland, came to our country to meet with the United States President George W. Bush.

The following day, Mr. Frank Shula, president of the Polish American Congress, arranged a "Welcome Gala Celebration" in the Chicago area to which hundreds of Polish-Americans were invited.

As president of the Hammond chapter of the Polish National Alliance, I was privileged to attend this elegant reception honoring President Kaczynski.

The date of this prestigious dinner party was February 10, 2006, exactly 66 years after February 10, 1940, when my family was abducted into Siberian slavery.

I have come a long way.

AFTERWORD

HISTORICAL PERSPECTIVE

Even though the following events took place earlier in history, the Polish deportees in this book did not know until many years later why and how they became unwilling pawns in two evil dictators' twisted global chess game.

In 1920 Russia invaded Poland as the first step of their objective to spread Communism to the whole world. In a battle known as the Miracle of the Vistulas, the Bolsheviks were defeated by the "blue" Polish army, which included Walter Zygmunt.

The Soviets did not give up on their goal to obliterate Poland, but were waiting for the right time and opportunity to exact their revenge.

In August of 1939, Russia and Germany signed the Ribbentrop-Molotov Pact, publicly pledging eternal friendship, but also secretly agreeing to divide Poland in half. As a nation, Poland was never supposed to exist again. Germany was to take the western half, and Russia would occupy the eastern part.

Right after the signing of the Ribbentrop-Molotov Pact, on September 1, 1939, German troops attacked Poland from the west. While Polish troops rushed to the western front, Russian troops came into Poland from the east later that month on the pretext of helping to defend the country against the Germans. In this way they attacked without declaring war. Poland's effective military resistance ended on October 2, 1939, and many of their aviators escaped to England to fight with the Royal Air Force against the German Luftwaffe. Lottie Zygmunt's future husband was one of these airmen.

Stalin's plan to get rid of the inhabitants of Poland was two-fold. The Soviet Union started its campaign to wipe Poland off the map of Europe by using deceit to lure army officers, priests, teachers, policemen and other leaders into Soviet territory. These 15,000 people were shot in the back of the head in a mass killing that became known as the Katyn Massacre. In this way many of Poland's defenders were eliminated.

The second part of Stalin's plan started in 1940 and 1941, when Russian troops broke into private homes at gunpoint to deport to Siberia hundreds of thousands of people from the eastern part of Poland, an area about 600 miles from north to south and 250 miles from east to west. They became slave laborers who were to be worked until they starved to death.

The number of people abducted is controversial. In his historically documented book, "When God Looked the Other Way," copyright, University of Chicago, 2004, Mr. Wesley Adamczyk examines the question of Polish deportee numbers. He explains in detail the reasoning of the Polish Academy of Science professors he interviewed.

The first deportees (including the Zygmunt family) were taken in February, 1940, when Russia transported these helpless people in cattle boxcars. In April of that year, thousands more were taken, and the third group was enslaved in June and July of that year. A fourth group was deported the next year. Russia gained two things from this evacuation: free slave labor and a way to steal the land of a third of Poland. Most of this area is now in Ukraine.

Geographical Siberia is in the Asian part of Russia. However, the labor camp of *Nizhnya Striga*, near Kotlas, was in the political Siberia. The captives were told they were in Siberia, even though the camp was not in Asia. It was about 150 miles north and 500 miles east of St. Petersburg, then known as Leningrad. Kotlas is about 300 miles south of the Arctic Circle.

The labor camps were spread all around Siberia to make it impossible for the slave workers to organize themselves, and these prisons were completely isolated from outside visitors. Other deportees were brought to small towns or communes where they were forced to live in inhumane conditions.

Strangely enough, Walter Zygmunt's family members were lucky they were among the first deportees to Russia. Their camp's warm barracks were already built for them when they got to *Nizhnya Striga*. There was a huge warm *banya* in which they could bathe once a week. Millie's family met some later deportees, who found themselves in prison camps without any kind of shelter. "Build it yourselves—after you have done your full day's work, of course."

When Russia was invaded by Germany on June 22, 1941, Stalin switched sides because he needed allies to help fight Germany. The treaty giving freedom to the Polish slaves was signed by Russia and the Polish government-in-exile on July 31,

1941. The able-bodied Polish men were released only to be required to join the British army. Because Germany occupied Poland, the former slave laborers could not go back to their homes in Poland.

Millie and her family were not told the news about their freedom until months later in October of 1941. Some of the Polish displaced persons may never have received this information.

Even then Stalin stubbornly called this agreement, to release the people he abducted, "an amnesty," thereby saying that these people were criminals who deserved to be imprisoned. Stalin had wanted to free only the young men strong enough for the army. The Polish and English governments demanded freedom for the older men, the women and the children too. Russia blamed Germany for the bad health of the newly freed slaves.

Again Walter's family was lucky to be among the first Polish people out of Siberia. The people of the southern provinces of Russia sympathized with them and found food and rough housing for them. They had a roof over their heads.

Some of the people coming later stayed outside in the elements, warm or cold, rain or shine. These former slaves came in such hordes that there wasn't enough of anything. Many of these malnourished people got out of Siberia only to die of starvation and disease in Kazakhstan or Uzbekistan at the door of freedom.

Many countries, like India and Mexico, accepted some of these displaced persons. The British built 22 Polish settlements in their colonies in Africa, which served a total population of 19,000 people. These camps housed 8000 young school children, 1500 adolescent girls, 3500 older men and 6000 women. Because the Polish teenaged boys went into military service at 14 or 15, there were few adolescent boys. Retired British Army officers commanded the camps, while the day-to-day management was in the hands of Polish officials.

Glossary

Foreign Words and Phrases

RUSSIAN

Mioca Ducha Switoho	Father Son and Holy Ghost
fufiaka	warm Russian coat
valenki	Russian sheep's wool felt boots with rubber soles
Manifesto	Communist constitution
banya	steam bath
Kto ne rabotaet, tot ne est	He who does not work, doesn't eat
Nizhnya Striga	the name of our prison camp
poselok	settlement-could be a village around a labor camp
NKVD	secret police-predecessor of KGB
Kopek or Kopeika	small Russian coin like a penny
dziesiatnik	payroll clerk, originally responsible for ten people
pud	old measurement meaning a heavy load
Udostowerenie	document allowing free movement to those previously held in prison camps
tovarisch	equal friend
svobodnyi grazhdanin	free citizen
magazin	shop with goods to sell
kolhoz	state-controlled commune or collective farm
svoloch	human scum
Krasnyi Ugolok	red corner, cultural center

eshelon   transport or railroad box-
                           cars carrying displaced
                           persons

POLISH

kal	shit, human waste
owsianka	soup made from water and cereal like oats
pluskwa	bedbug
kozaki	big edible mushrooms
nieludzka ziemia	inhuman earth
Polski Czerwony/Krzyz	Polish Red Cross
pupilka	ward (favorite nurse)
Sodalicja or Sodality	Polish religious organization for Catholic young people
Pulk Ulanow	Special unit of the regular Polish army
Paczkowy Bal	ball where they serve bismark rolls
wygnaniec	displaced person
krakowiak, polonez, kujawiak, polka, trojak	Polish dances
poprawiny	second day of wedding celebration
babcia	grandmother
dziadziu	grandfather
chrusciki	love knot pastry
Kot nie pracuje, ten nie je	He who doesn't work, doesn't eat

CPSIA information can be obtained at www.ICGtesting.com
Printed in the USA
LVOW131029190612

286769LV00001B/1/A